Spiritual Leadership for Women

Jeanie Shaw

Spiritual Leadership for Women

Spiritual Leadership for Women

© 2014 by Jeanie Shaw

All rights are reserved. No part of this book may be duplicated, copied, translated, reproduced or stored mechanically, digitally or electronically without specific, written permission of the author and publisher.

Printed in the United States of America.

ISBN: 978-1-939086-82-2

Unless otherwise indicated, all Scripture references are from the Holy Bible, New International Version, copyright 1973, 1978, 1984, 2011 by the International Bible Society. Used by permission of Zondervan Bible Publishers.

Cover and interior book design: Toney Mulhollan. The text face is set in Adobe Garamond Pro and Arial Narrow.

Illumination Publishers is committed to caring wisely for God's creation and uses recycled paper whenever possible.

Jeanie Shaw has served in the full-time ministry for forty years, working alongside her husband, Wyndham. For eight years Jeanie served as a vice president of HOPE *worldwide*. She has taught workshops and classes on marriage, parenting, loss, and leadership in numerous countries. She has four grown children, seven grandchildren, and two dogs. Her books include *Jacob's Journey, My Morning Cup, Understanding Goose, There's a Turkey at Your Door, Fruity Tunes and the Adventures of Rotten Apple,* and *Prime Rib.*

ILLUMINATION PUBLISHERS

www.ipibooks.com
6010 Pinecreek Ridge Court
Spring, Texas 77379-2513

*To our daughters and granddaughters,
as we strive to pass on the many valuable lessons
we have learned from spiritual women
who have gone before us.*

Contents

Acknowledgments	9
Introduction	11

Leadership and Character

1. Mary, Mother of Jesus: Leadership and Humility–Jeanie Shaw — **15**
Leadership Profile: Mary Allison, Santiago, Chile

2. Tabitha: Leadership and Example–Tammy Fleming — **22**
Leadership Profile: Rebecca Christensen, New Hampshire,

3. Hannah: Leadership and Vulnerability–Teresa Fontenot — **30**
Leadership Profile: Marcia Lamb, Massachusetts

4. Sarah: Leadership and Courage–Robin Williams — **39**
Leadership Profile: Corrina, Mumbai, India

5. The Sinful Woman: Leadership and Gratitude–Teresa Fontenot — **47**
Leadership Profile: Mealea Tan, Cambodia

6. The Bleeding Woman: Leadership and Faith–Jeanie Shaw — **54**
Leadership Profile: Ana Morrell, Edinburgh, Scotland

7. The Women in the Upper Room: Leadership and Prayer–Jeanie Shaw — **63**
Leadership Profile: Lena Johnson, London, England

Leadership and Competence

8. The Samaritan Woman: Leadership and Self-Awareness–Jeanie Shaw — **72**
Leadership Profile: Michelle Yaros, Missouri

9. Martha: Leadership and Hospitality–Teresa Fontenot — **79**
Leadership Profile: Ruby Ulm, London, England

10. Abigail: Leadership and Prudence–Jeanie Shaw — **87**
Leadership Profile: Catherine, Singapore

11. The Proverbs 31 Woman: Leadership and Organization–Robin Williams — **94**
Leadership Profile: Rachel Louis, Singapore

Contents

Leadership and Conviction

12. Esther: Leadership and Vision–Tammy Fleming **104**
Leadership Profile: Miki, China

13. The Canaanite Woman: Leadership and Boldness–Teresa Fontenot **113**
Leadership Profile: Amira Okundi, Nairobi, Kenya

14. Lydia: Leadership and Persuasion–Tammy Fleming **120**
Leadership Profile: Susan, New Delhi, India

15. Miriam: Leadership and Initiative–Jeanie Shaw **127**
Leadership Profile: Nadya Terzayn, Vinnytsia, Ukraine

16. Deborah: Leadership and Inspiration–Teresa Fontenot… **134**
Leadership Profile: Mariana Suiu, Bucharest, Romania

17. Mary of Bethany: Leadership that Doesn't Burn Out–Jeanie Shaw **142**
Leadership Profile: Norah Namei, Rwanda

18. Pharaoh's daughter: Leadership and Serving the Poor–Nadine Templer **149**
Leadership Profile: Jenny Blenko, La Paz, Bolivia and New York

Leadership and Chemistry

19. The Women of Romans 16: Leadership and Relationships–Jeanie Shaw **157**
Leadership Profile: Cristina Lombardi, Milan, Italy

20. Lois and Eunice: Leadership and Training–Jeanie Shaw **165**
Leadership Profile: Sarah Armstrong, Asunción, Paraguay and Florida

21. Ruth and Naomi: Leadership and Mentoring–Robin Williams **173**
Leadership Profile: Diddy Tempo Akello, Burundi

22. Euodia and Syntyche: Leadership and Conflict–Jeanie Shaw **181**
Leadership Profile: Jean Dziedzinski, Massachusetts

Contents

23. Hagar: Leadership Overcomes Dysfunction–Jeanie Shaw **188**
Leadership Profile: Terry Axe, Virginia

24. Priscilla: Leadership and Teamwork–Jeanie Shaw **197**
Leadership Profile: Pat Morr, International Missionary

Appendix **205**

Notes **211**

Acknowledgments

Numerous hearts and hands have gone into the writing of this book. My "fellow soldiers, fellow workers and dear friends" Teresa Fontenot, Robin Williams and Tammy Fleming were a joy to work with as they brought to life the leadership of several of the biblical women featured. Thank you.

Thank you to Nadine Templer for sharing a piece of her big heart for the poor in the chapter on Leadership and Serving the Poor. She also gathered many of the profiles of the women featured from around the world. I appreciate your tireless work. Thank you to the many elders' wives who contributed such valuable "pearls of wisdom" on leadership. You inspire and encourage me.

I also deeply appreciate the many spiritual women whose lives I have sought to imitate and learn from—I have watched you affect many lives for eternity as you follow Jesus. Thank you.

I'm very grateful for my editor, Elizabeth Thompson, who provides me with wise counsel, laughter and her wonderful way with words. A special thank you to my amazing husband and best friend, whose leadership is more like Jesus' than anyone I know. Thank you for being my greatest supporter and encourager—and for your patience on nights like tonight, when I am up much too late in order to finish "just one more chapter." I love you.

Introduction

I smiled at my two-year-old granddaughter as we shared a couple of cones in the neighborhood ice cream shop—mine coffee Heath Bar, hers chocolate. Though nearly sixty years span the gap between us, I basked in the joy of our relationship (and the scrumptious taste of the ice cream) as we sat and talked of princesses and pretty dresses.

Behind us, I overheard the giggly conversation of a group of young teen girls. They laughed about things they were Tweeting and took numerous "selfies" with their phones while they talked of things they liked and didn't like about themselves and others. As I wondered what might be taking place in the current story of their lives, I also mused about challenges and opportunities that might face these girls in the future—my chocolate-faced cherub included. I imagined these girls a few years down the road at a bar comparing notes about weekend parties and men they were with. Or even as a group of older women, graying and commiserating about aches and pains.

How will these girls, and the women they become, be able to navigate life and find a deeper meaning to sustain and propel them through the ups and downs?

Cultural challenges

We live in a challenging culture where women are pulled in many different directions. Magazines, movies, television, and online advertising tell us day after day that we are not smart enough, pretty enough, sexy enough, talented enough, or rich enough. We can feel the pressure to be "superwomen" who have it all—a thriving career, beautiful skin, designer clothes, buns of steel, Pinterest homes—while we lovingly watch our straight-A children float seamlessly from sports to art to drama and come home to a dinner of homemade animal-shaped organic pasta.

The pressure to conform to the world's view of womanhood is intense. But why is it so tempting? On any given day we can view the lives of "role models" from Hollywood whose lives have blown up as they live out the scripture in Isaiah 5:20–24:

> Woe to those who call evil good and good evil,
>   who put darkness for light and light for darkness,
>   who put bitter for sweet and sweet for bitter.

> Woe to those who are wise in their own eyes
>   and clever in their own sight.
> Woe to those who are heroes at drinking wine
>   and champions at mixing drinks,
> who acquit the guilty for a bribe,
>   but deny justice to the innocent.
> Therefore, as tongues of fire lick up straw
>   and as dry grass sinks down in the flames,
> so their roots will decay
>   and their flowers blow away like dust;
> for they have rejected the law of the LORD Almighty
>   and spurned the word of the Holy One of Israel.

Spiritual role models needed

A call to leadership is needed for women today. Who will stand tall? Who will lead the way? Who will show our little girls, our teenagers—women young and old—God's divine plan? Our world desperately needs women who will be an appealing contrast to today's distorted culture as they stand up on behalf of God's plan for women.

What about you? Will you make a difference? Will you practice spiritual leadership for women? While leadership is a gift from God, it can also be learned, cultivated, and strengthened. There are different types of leaders, and all are needed. You are needed. Perhaps you lead a large women's ministry or a very small group. Or maybe you work with youth or care for your grandchildren. You may open the Bible and your life with a friend or neighbor. You impact women around you more than you realize.

Overview of the book

The chapters in this book will take a peek into the lives of women from the Scriptures from whom we can learn leadership principles that transcend time and culture. Several other godly women I admire, who all have many years of leadership experience—Teresa Fontenot, Robin Williams, and Tammy Fleming—joined me in writing these chapters. Each of us has served in the ministry in various capacities—as women's ministry leaders, elders' wives, and servants—in churches large and small, all over the world. Altogether we have eight daughters and seventeen granddaughters. (Talk about motivation for passing on spiritual leadership principles to the next generation of women!) Interspersed throughout the book you will find quotes contributed from elders' wives around the globe, sharing biblical principles and practices they have learned in their years of experience.

The chapters will be followed with inspiring stories of modern-day women around the world who are inspiring others and making a difference for God. These women weren't necessarily trying to be leaders, but their lives have continually affected the lives of the people they touch. They illustrate true leadership in everyday life.

Because we follow Jesus, we have something wonderful to share. Women everywhere are waiting to be inspired by the amazing, life-changing message of Jesus. They are waiting to grow in their faith, to gain vision, and to see their womanhood be used to the glory to God.

Leadership

and

Character

CHAPTER ONE

Mary: Leadership and Humility
Jeanie Shaw
Luke 1

The anticipated day had arrived—Mary was betrothed. She had said yes to Joseph's offer of marriage by drinking the cup of wine he had poured for her. Her hands had trembled as she held the cup; her smile had made it difficult to swallow the wine. She had always thought Joseph was handsome, and she'd admired his strength of character. Her heart melted as he presented the gift he had made for her—a lovely wooden chest with her name carved on one side and his name on the other. Afterwards, in keeping with the custom of betrothals, he returned to his father's house to prepare a home for the two of them—and any children God might one day give them. They both knew that at just the right time, he would return for her.

Mary eagerly anticipated the shout that would come from Joseph's strong and familiar voice—a shout that would signify his nighttime arrival to take her to their home and consummate their marriage. With each sunset she wondered if this would be the night her groom would come. When he came, she and her bridesmaids would rush to grab their lanterns, giggling and squealing with excitement. She would veil her face and be led by a joyful procession to the wonderful place her groom had prepared for her—for *them*.

But then, in just one day and in one conversation with the angel Gabriel, everything changed. Her entire life was interrupted with God's plans. These plans would involve ridicule, pain, joy, misunderstanding, tears, and—as she would later learn from the prophet Simeon—a piercing of her very soul.

A faithful response

Mary's words to the angel Gabriel, "May it be to me as you have said," are a faithful response to a challenging and unexpected situation (Luke 1:38).

Mary was not hoping to be "held up" as an example of faith. She probably did not consider herself a leader among women. And yet her faithful response resulted in her becoming a leader—an example that women everywhere, from generation to generation, could look to for strength and inspiration.

What qualities in Mary's life caused God to choose her, out of all the women on earth, to carry his one and only Son? I believe he looked for a woman who loved the Scriptures, loved him, and was humble and contrite in heart. That's the kind of person God is always searching for (Isaiah 57:15; 2 Chronicles 16:9). *feeling or expressing remorse or penitence; affected by guilt.*

Mary understood that honoring God meant first being a servant. She did not consider herself entitled. Servants aren't entitled. She meditated on the Scriptures. She was happy to be used by God, even when her life's plans were interrupted.

As we see later in her life, she could get back up after she messed up. Mary succumbed at times to the temptation to be a controlling mother. In Matthew 12:46–50 we see her try to take charge of Jesus. This certainly makes her relatable to us, as we can also be tempted to "take charge of Jesus" by telling him how to be God in our lives.

She realized that loving Jesus meant loving his disciples when Jesus spoke these poignant words just before he died: "John, behold your mother. Dear woman, behold your son" (John 19:26–27).

She was loyal and stayed with Jesus to the end, and we again find her with him after his resurrection.

Whether we are full-time ministry leaders, small group leaders, or leaders among our children and friends, we can be inspired by Mary's life.

Humility is foundational.

Our own godly leadership must begin with the same foundation as Mary's. She was not striving to be a leader. She was a leader because of who she was. Her desire was to be known as God's servant. This meant she understood that he had the right to use her life as he saw best. He was the potter, she was the clay.

> The angel answered, "The Holy Spirit will come upon you, and the power of the Most High will overshadow you. So the holy one to be born will be called the Son of God. Even Elizabeth your relative is going to have a child in her old age, and she who was said to be barren is in her sixth month. For nothing is impossible with God."
>
> "I am the Lord's servant," Mary answered. "May it be to me as you have said." Then the angel left her. (Luke 1:35–38)

Mary believed God was big enough to do anything. She didn't say much in response to Gabriel's message. He had told her nothing was impossible for God, and she believed him. She believed even before she felt the baby move within her.

If we want to have a spiritual influence on other people, we must begin with the understanding that God is almighty and is big enough to do anything. He is our Creator. He knows things we don't know. His way will often make no sense to us. A spiritual leader surrenders to God's plan for her life. If we show people how great and almighty God is rather than how wise we think we are, we will be an inspiration to those around us.

"I am the Lord's servant. May it be to me as you have said" is a response we must strive to imitate. We will be called to serve God and his people in different ways throughout our lifetime—some of these ways will be without glory, and very few of them will be what we had planned. In every one of those times, we must decide all over again: How will we respond?

What kind of response would you have if all of your plans and dreams were uprooted and turned upside down? How do you respond now to tasks you are given? Are you concerned as to their "fairness"? Do you respond as a servant, or as one who feels entitled? When we feel we deserve leadership, we often feel "the rules" don't apply to us and that we deserve special treatment. Mary carried the Son of God and gave birth to him in a barn. She did not complain. She willingly and purposefully put herself under God's authority instead of telling God what he needed to do for her. We can miss the "I am the Lord's servant" attitude when we think that some ways we are asked to serve are "beneath us."

We can also miss the power of God when we think we can't do what God asks of us—it's just too difficult. "Nothing is impossible with God" and "I am the Lord's servant. May it be to me as you have said" will always prove to be responses that influence others for good.

Even though Mary was astonished by the course her life took, she was also spiritually prepared for the life God called her to lead. She showed that she understood the Scriptures and promises of God as she wove them throughout her song of praise and thanksgiving in Luke 1:46–55. Our study and understanding of the Scriptures prepares us for the challenges we face. It also gives us wisdom as we interact with others. A person who knows and uses the Scriptures possesses a leadership component incomparable to those who rely on their own wisdom or the world's wisdom. Are you still studying the Scriptures? Are they the basic tools you use as you lead?

Mary found joy in the price of her calling. She could have approached her life with a "grin and bear it" attitude, or even a martyr's spirit. Like her son after her, she was "despised and rejected" by many (Isaiah 53:3). However, her response to God's plan for her life was one of joy. Yes, at times she had a broken heart, but the joy of serving God was foundational to her responses. As you serve in the various roles and responsibilities you have, do you find joy in the price? Are you delighted to be used by God, or do you complain about your circumstances and hardships? If you become negative, few will want to follow in your footsteps. Who wants to join in someone's complaining spirit? Mary's attitude toward serving God is contagious as she begins her song:

> "I'm bursting with God-news;
>   I'm dancing the song of my Savior God.
> God took one good look at me, and look what happened—
>   I'm the most fortunate woman on earth!
> What God has done for me will never be forgotten."
> (Luke 1:46–48, the Message Bible)

Women everywhere want this kind of song in their hearts!

- Ask people around you if humility is evident in your life.
- Does it show by your willingness to serve in all kinds of areas?
- Does it show in your ongoing eagerness to keep learning from the Scriptures?
- Does it show as you step out in faith in areas beyond your comfort zone?
- Do you feel honored to have God's Spirit living in you? Or do you rely on your own power?
- Do you live your Christian life as if it is a burden or a joyful privilege?

If roller coasters had been invented before Mary lived, she may have likened her life to a ride on a coaster. The rolls and turns were terrifying and exhilarating—sometimes both at once. Mary knew what it meant to feel utterly blessed, and she knew what it felt like to have a sword pierce her soul. And yet she humbly and gratefully embraced her journey with Jesus, mourning beneath his cross when he died, and praising God when he arose. As your walk with God unfolds, you too will face the unexpected and the unimaginable. But as you face the thrills and defeats that come your way, may your heart reflect Mary's humility, and sing her song of faith.

There is no godly leadership without humility! My lifelong challenge is to "be completely humble" (Ephesians 4:2). It is one thing to be humble with some people, in some circumstances, but it is another thing altogether to be completely humble. It is humbling to know how much I must rely on God!
—Gloria Baird, Los Angeles, California

Jesus describes himself as "lowly in heart." No wonder humility is a qualification for entering his kingdom. Whenever I get bent out of shape, it is usually because I am not being lowly—toward God, or toward people.
—Mary Lou Craig, Boonton, New Jersey

As leaders we need to model openness and vulnerability in our relationships so that others may see humility in action. Teaching about humility and practicing it are two different things.
—Caron Vassallo, Melbourne, Australia

There is no leadership without humility. Humility brings with it vulnerability and trust. Without trust, people will not follow.
—Sally Hooper, Dallas, Texas

I believe humility is one of the most difficult Christlike qualities to attain. Hopefully, as I am made more into his likeness I will inch my way towards humility. The older I get, the easier it is to feel I know what I am doing—or to let self-righteousness rear its ugly head. I think of the scripture "with the measure you use, it will be measured to you" (Luke 6:38) and think of the grace I will need on judgment day. I will try to humbly extend that grace to others, as well as keep on praying the Lord's Prayer, asking for forgiveness for me first—and then forgiving others.
—Karen Louis, Singapore

Romans 12:3 tells us, "Don't think of yourself more highly than you ought"— or in other words, "Don't believe your own press." This is difficult, because as leaders, we need encouragement from those we lead. Often, the only way we know if our words or efforts are getting through is by the verbal responses coming back to us. We need encouragement, it "makes our work a joy" (Hebrews 13:17), and it tells us if we have, in fact, helped. On the other hand, we have to remain humbly sobered by who we really are—our strengths and our very real weaknesses. It is great to be encouraged, but we can't allow Satan to convince us that we are better than we are. Instead, let us count it a privilege and a blessing to be used by God, fully aware of our own constant need to grow and change. None of us has arrived!
—Geri Laing, Lake Worth, Florida

PROFILE

Mary Allison, Santiago, Chile: Humility
by Mary Allison

As a college student, Mary Allison came to love her God, and she has served him wholeheartedly ever since. Whether she is serving in her home country (the United States), helping women in India and Afghanistan, or spending her empty-nester years on the mission field and learning a new language, Mary exemplifies humility. Like her namesake, Mary the mother of Jesus, she embodies the role of "the Lord's servant."

Mary is a "young" sixty-year-old grandmother, now leading the women's ministry in Santiago, Chile. As you read the lessons she shares from her life in Christ, you'll see why she's such an example of humility in leadership:

While I was a freshman at the University of Florida, I met people from the Crossroads Church of Christ, and learned so much about what it meant to follow the Bible. From the time I first read the New Testament, I knew there was nowhere else where I would find a genuine standard for my life and find friends that would help me get to heaven. Did I wake up one morning and decide I was going to move to India, Afghanistan, the Middle East, or Chile? No. As a matter of fact, I had been raised in only one city (Miami) until I left for college, and I had lived most of those years in the same house. But when the Bible became my standard, I learned to view the world through new eyes. Now I focus on doing what God wants me to do and allowing him to direct my steps. It is God who has taken us to so many different places, not me.

You might wonder if I knew before I married my husband that one day I would live in many exotic places. The answer, again, is a very clear no. Change can be scary. Many of us shy away from it all together. But I learned to like it and even to look for opportunities to change. But this didn't come easily.

In 1986, we went to India with the church planting. I was so scared when we landed, and I felt like I was drowning for a while. Only my relationships and prayer kept my head above water. Each decision along the way had to be met with prayer, advice, and more prayer.

In staying strong with God, I have come to realize that Bible study is crucial. Sometimes I spend months listening to the Word while exercising. I focus on a particular book and write notes on what I am learning. I read a book, and then read it again after a few months. I am particularly encouraged when I find parallel passages to whatever I am reading. I don't claim to be any kind of scholar—I am just trying to learn as much as I can when I read. I gain so much from the work of others. I listen to messages and distill them, and sometimes send the notes to my children. All of this said, I am on a constant quest to learn more. I love it every time I learn something new, so I try to make my Bible study a daily part of my life.

It's important to me that I don't become so safe and comfortable in my life that I forget that the majority of the world doesn't live that way. Being careful not to love my surroundings or things too much keeps me ready to move.

The church has always been my safe place. Each year I grow deeper in my understanding of why Jesus referred to us as sheep. It's an amazing and profound analogy for us. In most passages about sheep, perhaps Jesus is more talking about himself as the shepherd and how dependent and in need of his protection we are. So when we as sheep get into trouble, we need him (through the church) to rescue us. And we will need this again and again. I am so thankful for the many churches I have been a part of in our family of churches. Wherever I go around the world, I am loved and cared for by God's people.

Perhaps I have just scratched the surface of many things. I pray for you to have as rich a life in Christ as I have had—learning, repenting, changing, and being challenged.

CHAPTER TWO

Tabitha: Leadership and Example

Tammy Fleming

Acts 9:36-43

Her back ached as she leaned over the spindle. Her calloused hands carefully wove the threads that would soon become a garment. As Tabitha tired, she thought of the women who needed these clothes, picturing their joy as they received them and held them close. This thought motivated her to keep on working. She loved that she was able to meet needs of these women, most of whom were widows. She would receive no money for her labor—the smiles on the faces of the women who wore them would be payment enough. No one asked her to serve in this way. She did it for one reason—love. She loved God and loved people. This love produced in her a lifestyle that kept on giving.

Tabitha, one of only a handful of individuals raised from the dead in the New Testament, "was abounding with deeds of kindness and charity" (Acts 9:36, New American Standard Bible).

If we imagine her life as a white artist's canvas, every part of her would have been covered with good deeds, painted over from edge to edge in the brilliant colors of her kindness and work for the poor. If we think about her soul, it was permeated with good deeds. The Greek word used here, *pleres*, indicates that she was full of good deeds; God's testimony about her is that she was lacking nothing—she was perfect, in the sense of being complete in doing good to others and serving the poor.[1] It seems that she took every opportunity to serve others and meet the needs of people around her.

One might ask, Was a woman like Tabitha considered a leader among the disciples in the nascent Christian church? Tabitha's kind of humble, behind-the-scenes service is not always considered a form of leadership—unfortunately, it can sometimes escape notice in the church, and it is certainly undervalued in the world.

A couple of years ago, I had the opportunity to study the Bible with Chidz, a brilliant economics student from the United Kingdom's University of

Birmingham; Chidz has become a dear and precious friend. As she was studying the Scriptures and learning what it means to truly follow Jesus, she got invited to a weeklong internship, sponsored by a leading firm among the Fortune 500 companies. It was The Place to Be for the top twenty or so young black leaders in the UK. What an honor to be invited! It was a week of workshops and keynote speeches by directors and CEOs from the likes of Google, investment banks, and other top employers. Participants were given tasks to complete, in groups and individually. The aim of the internship was to paint a picture of what it means to be a leader in today's world. The various guest speakers talked about the cost of success: choosing to put career before personal and family life in order to get ahead; striving to be the best among their staff and employees; finding and creating new strategies for personal development so you stand out in a highly competitive field. It became clear to Chidz that success was evaluated in terms of how high you could climb on the scale of accumulated wealth and status.

During one evaluation, when the participants were doing individual presentations on the topic "What is a leader," Chidz used Jesus as her model, and talked about the quality of servanthood. Her team leader, who was famous for being one of the creators of the Cloud, roundly rejected her idea, saying this philosophy of "others first" was the mark of a weak leader, not an effective leader. Chidz was floored by this, and came home rather stunned at how diametrically opposed the world's concept of leadership, as presented in this workshop, was from what inspired her to follow Jesus.

The word *leader* (literally "one who rules" in the NIV) only appears five times in the New Testament in reference to those within the church.[2] The only time Jesus is recorded as using the word is in Luke 22:26, when he says, "the greatest among you should be like the youngest, and the one who rules [or the leader] like the one who serves." In contrast, the word *servant* (with its associated forms of *service* and to *serve*) occurs sixty times in the New Testament in reference to those within the church.[3] Jesus defines this term through his personal example and his teaching: he who was the greatest leader of all time was the greatest servant. Jesus, "being in very nature God, did not consider equality with God something to be grasped, but made himself nothing, taking the very nature of a servant [literally *slave*]" (Philippians 2:6–7, NIV).

Tabitha is introduced to us as a disciple and as a great servant. She was following Jesus, exquisitely. Her identity and example as a faithful follower of Jesus should impress upon us the fact that humble servanthood is an essential quality of a leader.

Tabitha's ministry was not glamorous. Those gathered at her deathbed were not the rich and famous, but the poor and destitute. How did she find the spiritual energy to keep on serving a needy group of people? I know I sometimes find myself worrying about what investing more energy in people will take away from me—time? Money? Somehow, Tabitha did not fall into the trap of deficit-thinking—focusing on all the things that are not—and did not worry about what might happen to her if she let the needs of the people around her encroach upon her personal space.

Tabitha didn't seem to have a husband, older brother, or father in her home, yet she found something very good and productive that she could do for God, and she got on with it—for a while, anyway. And then, the further spiritual implications of her story must not escape us: she grew weak; she got sick; her illness was so serious that she actually *died*. Have you ever felt dead spiritually? Drained absolutely dry? What did it take for Tabitha to be revived?

I remember feeling this way during a time of difficulty in one of the churches we served. It seemed like everyone in the church was going through a hard time, and I was exhausted. Without realizing it, I stopped looking at the facts with faith, and had gone flat —and I couldn't see it until my husband brought it up to me.

I knew that the first thing I needed to examine was the quality of my relationship with God. I had to admit that there were days when I got out of bed and launched immediately into answering e-mail or serving my family or doing the dishes from the night before, and reduced my time with God to a brief, legalistic check-in. I had to face the fact that *I was the one stealing faith from myself*—my circumstances weren't to blame.

The entrance of Peter into Tabitha's crisis, and God working through Peter, was the game-changer. "When the disciples heard that Peter was in Lydda, they sent to men to him and urged him, 'Please come at once!' " (Acts 9:38). The disciples could have just accepted that God had called their sister Tabitha home to heaven, and been comforted in their loss by the knowledge that she had died saved. For some reason, this is not what they did. They issued a desperate cry for help and sent for Peter.

I remember a conversation I once had with spiritual friends, as they were listening to me rattle off a long list of the numerous challenges in my life. After expressing genuine empathy and concern, they also said, "We've heard *that* story. What we need now is a *faith* story." I had to realize that I am the one in control of whether or not I face my circumstances with faith. While this felt a bit humiliating, it was also a tremendous relief—because, like the disciples in Joppa, with all my heart I also longed for a solution and the miracle of a resurrection out of my dead-end thinking. Ironically, while God promises that "his divine power has given us everything we need for life and godliness" (2 Peter 1:3), I could never have resurrected my faith on my own. I needed to be pointed to Christ. I believe that churches and individuals need strong, loving, consistent, encouraging friendships with peers, advisors, and those qualified to help and strengthen our faith, when circumstances become desperate.

Who would have guessed that sewing clothes for people would be the example of Christ's love that the disciples in Joppa just couldn't live without! Be careful not to disqualify the sincere signs of Jesus' love and compassion that we each can give to one another, regarding them as gifts of little value. Don't underestimate the importance of "small acts," like spending time in the homes of women in church whom we don't know so well; inviting others into our own homes; and being careful to remember the poor and needy in a personal and consistent way. Tabitha teaches us that our way of life affects others in ways we may not see or understand on this side of life. Our example lives on in the lives of others even after we die. It's interesting that we don't see Tabitha having trained anyone to do what she did. When she died, it seems there was no one ready to stand in the gap and provide the same service that she provided. Who knows—maybe this was the instruction Peter gave the little church after raising her from the dead. Or perhaps other women, as they thought about Tabitha's example, were inspired to carry on the loving acts of kindness she had offered them. Either way, she had a lasting impact on the people whose lives she touched, and her life still serves as an inspiring example for all who read her story today.

- Why is the example you set an important leadership quality?
- Do you tend to equate servanthood with leadership? If so, how can you practice servant leadership?
- What does Jesus say about those who teach or lead others but aren't concerned about the example their life sets?
- Are you aware of the example you set in the way you serve others? The way you pray? The way you share your faith? The way you speak . . . ? If so, what would your example show about the love in your heart for God and people?
- If you are not aware of how others see the example of your life, how might you become more aware?

Like Tabitha, let us all strive to set an example for the people around us—our family, our friends, our neighbors, our family in Christ. We don't need an impressive title or lots of money to change the world. Tabitha shows us that even small acts make a big difference.

The Apostle Paul always reminded people that they knew how he had lived among them. He was transparent. The godly life not only validates a leader's teaching—it is a lesson in itself.

—Linda Brumley, San Diego, California

"An ounce of prevention is worth a pound of cure." I often use this familiar saying to remind others that it's the small things we do each day, each week, and throughout the year that add up to amazing things in your marriage, parenting, relationships, health, etc.

—Laura Fix, Londonderry, New Hampshire

The best example to set is the example of how to repent. Then people will always know how to correct the mistakes they learned from you.

—Teresa Fontenot, Sydney, Australia

Hypocrisy is the stumbling block that has kept too many of our children from becoming Christians. The importance of being a great example to people in the world and to our brothers and sisters in Christ cannot be overstated. If we are not living the lifestyle of a disciple of Jesus, our children will be the first to notice. The consequences of hypocrisy can be eternal for both parents and children—a price no one wants to pay.

—Nancy Mannel, Los Angeles, California

I learned a lot from Jesus' leadership in how to lead by first setting a personal example. Two simple words in Acts 1:1¬–2—do and teach—remind me what I need to do first. It is so true that actions can speak louder than words. One great example from Jesus was when he washed his disciples' feet to show the full extent of his love. He then taught them to do likewise.

—Elizabeth Sinn, Hong Kong, China

PROFILE

Rebecca Christensen, New Hampshire: Example
by Laura Fix, New Hampshire

This article was written seven years ago. Rebecca Christensen passed from this life on December 27, 2013. Though she could no longer talk near the end of her life, she found ways to communicate her gratitude for God and for those around her. Even after her death, men and women have been moved to draw closer to God as a result of the way she lived and died. As more than four hundred people shared in a celebration of Rebecca's life, her impact was evident and her legacy remains rich and deep. As family members and friends who Rebecca had brought to God shared about her, it was clear that her life had changed many lives. Her husband and adult children shared of her faith. Her daughter Jenna recounted a conversation where she had asked her mom, "Why you, Mom?" Rebecca had simply replied, "Why not me?" She gracefully accepted the good and the difficult with faith.

I'd like to tell you about my friend Rebecca Christensen. Rebecca is fifty years old, has been married to her husband, Carl, for more than half her life, and together they have three wonderful teenage children. Rebecca became a Christian in 1985 and has faithfully served the Lord in various leadership roles, including the full-time ministry, for a number of years. While these facts about Rebecca are impressive, they only provide a glimpse of why she inspires so many women.

In 2005 Rebecca noticed something was wrong. While driving home one day, she passed out behind the wheel. The family van was damaged, but she was spared any major injuries. She was taken to the hospital for evaluation. The reason for her losing consciousness was elusive. The typical battery of tests revealed little. More specialized tests were ordered.

As time passed, she noticed a slight tremble in her hand. Soon after, her arm began to shake and her once clear speech began to slur. She knew she was deteriorating, but she didn't know why. Tests indicated she had Multiple

System Atrophy (MSA) Parkinsonism. MSA has a life-expectancy of less than ten years once diagnosed. There is no remission or cure.

The physical battle, coupled with constant uncertainty, began affecting other areas of her life. Her daily household duties became increasingly difficult, if not impossible. She loved to prepare meals for her family, but over time, due to loss of strength in her right arm and hand, she couldn't even manage to butter toast. Planting flowers, one of her favorite seasonal hobbies, had to be done by others. Rebecca couldn't walk unaided, and soon became restricted to a wheelchair. It wasn't long before she lost the use of her right arm. She could no longer get dressed or turn the pages of a book. The simple task of putting herself to bed became a family affair.

The emotional battle, over time, became equally daunting. Thoughts crept into her mind: "Will I see my children get married?" and "Why is this happening to me?" The struggles of feeling useless and burdensome, along with the pain of watching her husband add her responsibilities to his already full schedule, were ever-present.

From her first diagnosis, Rebecca was faced with a choice: She could trust God's hand in her life, or she could give into fear, bitterness, and self-pity. While her choice would need to be made on a daily basis, she decided to humbly accept God's plan for her life and be an overcomer, no matter the situation. Rebecca stated, "I want to focus on what I can become for God, realizing that no matter what disease does to my body, I have my relationship with God. When I face moments of being overwhelmed I ask God for his comfort."

And the God of all comfort responded in a very real way. Rebecca began to notice that comfort took a form she didn't expect—the form of a peace and joy that "washes over me." She went on to say, "Oddly, for the first time in over twenty-four years as a disciple, I realize that God has individually chosen me. Of course I heard it all before, but this time I felt a deeper confidence that it was true—that God had reached out to me through a disciple and enabled me to respond to the gospel message. For about a month I marveled at the notion, holding on to an overwhelming sense of security and gratefulness. This God who chose me could be trusted with my best interest. What encourages me so much is that I have so many wonderful friends praying for me. I want to be an encouragement and example to them and be someone who is faithful and positive through this time."

Rebecca's daughter Jenna, shared, "Sometimes she's sad. Sometimes she's tired. But she doesn't lose hope. Her Bible is always open. She's still growing. I can visibly see how God is moving in her heart just from looking at the growth in our own relationship. If I have a problem with a friend or an issue I'm facing, a solution can be remedied by her words."

Rebecca once hosted a women's Bible discussion in her home. Women she met from around the community would come and study the Bible together. She can no longer do this, yet those same women stop by with meals, offer to do errands, or simply lend a hand with household chores. They have been inspired, not just by the things she taught from God's word, but from the life she lives.

Rebecca has taught me so much about faithfulness, hope, and gratitude when circumstances are extremely difficult. One of her favorite scriptures to share is Romans 15:13: "May the God of hope fill you with all joy and peace as you trust in him, so that you may overflow with hope by the power of the Holy Spirit."

CHAPTER THREE

Hannah: Leadership and Vulnerability

Teresa Fontenot

1 Samuel 1-2

For Hannah, it was one more year to travel up to Shiloh to worship and sacrifice to the Lord—one more year with empty arms and an aching heart. Her husband, Elkanah, was a devout man who never failed to make this pilgrimage. Elkanah was a devoted father and husband, and unlike many other men, he made this journey with his entire family, which included his two wives, Hannah and Peninnah, and all of Peninnah's sons and daughters. He shared the sacrificial meal with them, and they worshiped together as a family. This they did, year after year.

Despite Elkanah's best efforts to lead his family righteously, disappointment and strife simmered under his roof. Hannah was barren. Even though Hannah was very secure in her husband's love, "the Lord had closed her womb" (1 Samuel 1:5). Her barrenness was a social embarrassment for her husband, and although he could have divorced her, he remained lovingly devoted to her. Hannah felt her failure to conceive intensely. Her husband's love, combined with Peninnah's gloating, only increased the pressure Hannah felt to bear a child. Hannah was ridiculed in her own home. Even as Hannah tried to worship God, Peninnah provoked her "till she wept and would not eat" (v. 7). Her rival wife used every opportunity to remind Hannah that she was under a curse. Undoubtedly, Peninnah's children learned to mock Hannah as well. Life was miserable for her.

Elkanah's attempts to fix the situation—giving her double portions of the sacrificial meat and reminding her of his faithful love—were also painful. Hannah appreciated his efforts, but they only made things worse. How could a man understand these things? She couldn't explain to him the longing of her empty arms. He could never understand the depths of her feelings. He could not fully share her struggle. There was only one place she could go.

Hannah's transformation

Despite the fact that she had prayed thousands of prayers begging God for a child, Hannah would not give up and would not give in to the hardening that threatened her heart. She was vulnerable to the criticalness of others, but she did not retreat or retaliate. She was desperate, but she knew where to turn. She would not close up and protect her wounded heart. Hannah would not believe that she was wasting her time by trusting in God. God's silence did not mean that he was not at work. She would simply open her heart wider than ever before. Hannah would pour out all the tears and pain stored up in her soul. She would cry until she had no more tears. She would pray out her bitterness and surrender her deepest desires to God alone, holding nothing back in her spiritual worship. Her face dripped with tears and her mouth moved fervently as she made her vow to God: "In bitterness of soul Hannah wept much and prayed to the Lord" (v. 10).

Once again, Hannah was misunderstood. Eli, the priest, rebuked Hannah for being a drunkard. Hannah had good reason to become discouraged and bitter. She was unable to bear children; she shared her husband with a woman who ridiculed her; her loving husband could not solve her problems; and even the high priest misunderstood her motives. It was a test of vulnerability—would she tell Eli the truth, or hide the reasons for her suffering?

Hannah, however tempted she must have been, did not give in to frustration and anger. Nor did she give in to hopelessness. She again opened her heart with the hope that the priest would understand. She did not walk away annoyed or defeated; she shared her feelings of "great anguish and grief" (v. 16). Hannah had the vulnerability and willingness to be misunderstood. She chose to be honest, and shared her heart in the midst of her pain, not waiting until she could make herself more presentable. Hannah did not apologize for her grief or her appearance. She stated clearly and respectfully what was in her heart. She was not afraid of sharing her honest feelings.

Hannah was not so overcome with emotion that she lost perspective on her life as the servant to an all-powerful God. Hannah had no intention of being an example to you or me about vulnerability, openness, or prayer. I'm sure she would have never called herself a leader. Hannah was open because she was compelled to be. The cost of holding her anguish and bitterness in would have been her very soul. She had to come to a place of surrender.

Asking of others makes us vulnerable. Hannah was not too proud or too afraid to passionately ask God for a child. She also asked Eli for his blessing.

Hannah, of course, went on to have a son, Samuel, who became a prophet, the last judge, a deliverer, and the man who anointed the first and second kings of Israel.

As time went on, Hannah continued to live a life of vulnerability. She fulfilled her vow and entrusted her little son to God, with Elkanah's permission.

Hannah left Samuel under the care of Eli, whose track record as a father was a bit dubious. Then she left Ramah, childless once again. From then on, she saw her son only once a year and presented him with a robe she had spent all year lovingly stitching for him. Hannah's every act was one of vulnerability, opening her heart to joy and to pain. The Bible has preserved for us Hannah's beautiful prayer of thanksgiving (1 Samuel 2:1–10), which is similar in many ways to the prayer of Jesus' mother, Mary, another vulnerable and trusting woman of God (Luke 1:46–55).

Vulnerable women practice gratitude. Hannah's psalm radiates joy and the triumph of God. She was talking to God, and at the same time talking to herself—telling herself the truth about him. Surely as Samuel grew, he learned from his mother's example, and took her theology with him as he ministered to God's people and to kings.

The value of vulnerable leadership

Vulnerable and *leadership* are not usually two words we put together. We think of leaders as being strong and confident. The apostle Paul learned to embrace God's concept of leadership:

> But he said to me, "My grace is sufficient for you, for my power is made perfect in weakness." Therefore I will boast all the more gladly about my weaknesses, so that Christ's power may rest on me. That is why, for Christ's sake, I delight in weaknesses, in insults, in hardships, in persecutions, in difficulties. For when I am weak, then I am strong. (2 Corinthians 12:9–10)

God's way is for us to lead with transparency, honesty, and vulnerability. Mother Teresa once said, "Honesty and transparency make you vulnerable. Be honest and vulnerable anyway."

The test of transparency

Openness is scary. Openness is essential. It is essential for every disciple, and is a practice we cannot neglect when we begin to lead others. When we become leaders, Satan loves to tempt us with the desire to hide our sins and weaknesses so that we will always look good and never disappoint the people following us. How quickly do you confess sin, admit mistakes, and take responsibility? Don't forget that when light shines on anything, it brings purity and power. As leaders, we should be the first to admit our mistakes, confess our sins, and do whatever is necessary to make things right. As Hebrews 4:13 reminds us, "Nothing in all creation is hidden from God's sight."

Openness requires courage. In the past, the word *courage* was connected to the inmost thoughts and feelings.[4] Learn to be courageous and vulnerable in the areas where you are most insecure. There is a freedom that comes from transparency. Fear and insecurity can bind us and keep us from leading in faith. Those of us who are more fearful and insecure must make efforts to be even more open. If we don't, we become trapped in ourselves and anxious that people will find out "who we really are," and we are plagued by the fear "What will they think of me?"

We must be open, or we will become self-absorbed and unable to connect. Being genuine brings us back to a common ground with others that creates bonding and trust in our leadership. And consider this: our openness encourages others to share their fears. It helps us, and the people who we influence, to realize that we are all human and dependent upon God's grace to make us more than we really are. How open are you with the people you are close to? With your family? When you speak or teach others? Have you trained yourself in this area so that it has become a natural part of who you are and how you lead?

"Don't waste your suffering." If you've ever heard my friend Gloria Baird speak, perhaps you've heard her say this. How right she is! This saying reflects the wisdom and inspiration of Hannah. As disciples, we are forever learning. Our life as leaders is a process whereby God continues to train, refine, prune, and test us. We are always learning, growing, discovering, and changing. Take people with you on that journey! As we share our challenges and the lessons we are gaining from them, other people will benefit from our experiences, and get to know us better in the process. And something special happens along the way: We begin to journey together with the same heart.

The pain Hannah expressed made her joy that much sweeter. Do the women you are leading know what you are learning right now? Do they feel a part of your journey?

Dr. Brené Brown, a leading researcher on vulnerability, courage, worthiness, and shame, wrote, "Vulnerability sounds like truth and feels like courage. Truth and courage aren't always comfortable, but they're never weakness."[5]

Just ask!

We are leaders because we like to help others. But being vulnerable means that we must also allow others to help us. If we are willing to admit areas of weakness, then it naturally follows that we should let other people use their strengths. Can you admit that you don't know how to do something and ask someone to help you? If you can't make something happen, are you comfortable asking someone else to do it? So many times, we don't want to appear weak or stupid or incompetent, so we don't ask. Even when we feel incompetent or ill-equipped to do something, we just tell ourselves, "I'm supposed to be able to do this," or "I'm the only one who *can* do this." Usually, neither one of these statements is true; we just need to ask for help! And even if those statements do hold some truth, how can we learn what we are supposed to do, or train other people to do it, if we don't work together? This is where vulnerability comes in.

If we will let it, vulnerability can give us a healthy self-awareness. A great pitfall in leadership is taking ourselves too seriously. We think (perhaps unconsciously), "I'm the only person who can do this. Without me, the whole thing will come crashing down." But vulnerability reminds us that God is all-powerful, and he can work through anyone, any way he chooses. Although we are all important to him and useful to him, no one is indispensable. As we live transparently before others, we are reminded that we are only clay vessels.

Understanding our weakness helps us not take ourselves too seriously. Learn to laugh at your "cracks" instead of being surprised by them. People love it when we share our most embarrassing moments. Would your friends say this is a strength for you? How can you learn to laugh more freely at yourself?

Vulnerability and openness must come from a sincere heart. Hannah's openness was not a means to an end. She was not trying to dump her problems on Eli or gain sympathy from him. She did not share her situation as an excuse to stay weak. Hannah genuinely felt grief, shared it, and received the blessing she asked for. In our openness, we must always guard against self-pity. Hannah's desire to surrender her child to the Lord removed the self-pity from her heart. She completely trusted God with her lot. If Hannah had never had a child, she would have remained a woman of faith because she sought God from the depth of her despair. Hannah opened herself to the greatest joy and the greatest sacrifice she could imagine.

Hannah remains an upward call to us. Her life is a beautiful example of the ways that faith and openness go hand in hand. Her journey to trust God with both her present and her future, through good times and bad, is one we can all learn from as we navigate our own journeys. Let us learn to live openly, honestly, and without fear, inviting God and other people along. As we do this, we will become women who please God and help others, even as we learn to "laugh at the days to come" (Proverbs 31:25).

- Do you pray openly until you get down to the hurt, and then pray through it? Hannah's prayers of both despair and joy teach us to learn to express the full gamut of our emotions.

- Are you comfortable with asking for help from others? Think of some areas where you are reluctant to ask for help, and identify the people you can approach.
- How do you respond when you feel misunderstood? When you are provoked or discouraged? These are the moments when it can be most difficult to remain vulnerable and open.
- How willing are you to let people see you in your most desperate moments? Too often we want to clean ourselves up, then discuss things in a more civilized manner later.
- How do you relate to the concept of vulnerability in leadership? Do you embrace it? Resist it? Both?
- Where might you want to be more vulnerable in your work life or personal life? What steps can you take to do that?

Let us open our hearts to God and to people. Vulnerability allows us to live in freedom, confidence, and truth. Vulnerability turns us into the kind of women and leaders God can use—*real* women, *real* leaders. Real people like Hannah, who lived openly and honestly, and whose struggles and triumphs have encouraged generations of women.

Vulnerability can be challenging because it means exposing ourselves to possible criticism. It takes effort, humility, and trust in God's unconditional love to be vulnerable. When I am vulnerable, people say they are glad to know me better, they feel that I am more relatable, and they have more hope for their own lives.

—Mary Lou Craig, Boonton, New Jersy

If you are afraid for anyone to know about you, be the first to tell them about you.

—Teresa Fontenot, Sydney, Australia

Don't waste your pain. God disciplines those he loves, but when we experience hard things it does not always mean that we will learn the lessons that God wants us to learn. We must beg God to train us so we will not waste our pain, but through our pain train others so that they can avoid our mistakes. This takes both self-awareness and vulnerability.

—Kim Evans, Philadelphia, Pennsylvania

Vulnerability is defined in the dictionary as weakness, but it takes great strength and courage to be vulnerable.

—Virginia Lefler, Chicago, Illinois

I look at being vulnerable as (a) being able to press my pause button when my emotions are triggered by something or someone, and (b) distilling it all down to what my most childlike/vulnerable side needs/wants/feels, then (c) expressing it with humility, gentleness and courage in an endearing way—not an "off-putting" way. It is not easy to practice or to teach, but I believe it is what Jesus is looking for when he says, "Except we become like a little child, we will not enter the kingdom of heaven" (Luke 18:17).

—Karen Louis, Singapore

The Bible is rich with stories of men and women who have sinned. I believe God gave us these examples so we could relate, see his love for us, and have hope. When counseling other women, I have learned that the more open, vulnerable, and compassionate I am, the more relatable I become—trust is built and hope is given.

—Nancy Mannel, Los Angeles, California

PROFILE

Marcia Lamb, Massachusetts: Vulnerability

by Jeanie Shaw, Massachusetts

She sees herself as a "cracked vessel"—vulnerable to breakage. But this vulnerability is precisely what creates so much of the uniqueness, beauty, and strength she exhibits. My friend Marcia Lamb has experienced challenges and trials in her life that would tempt many to fall apart under the pressure. Yet Marcia continues to grow stronger. The "refining through fire" that she has experienced has strengthened the vessel—and made it a thing of beauty.

While Marcia was still a young mother, her middle child was diagnosed with leukemia on his sixth birthday. Given little chance for survival, Michael began a three-year treatment of chemotherapy. Amazingly, her son overcame and was pronounced cancer-free several years later.

Marcia's husband was a minister, and over the years this calling often put the family "on display." Marcia didn't run from the fishbowl, but learned to let God use it for his glory. They moved often throughout their years in the ministry as they helped numerous churches. It is difficult to move when life is running "smoothly." It is even more difficult when you must uproot an already unsettled situation and again open your heart to new relationships. Marcia made a decision to continue to open her heart and "bloom where she was planted."

Then came her turn to face the dreaded disease—cancer. Shortly after Michael was pronounced cured, Marcia herself was diagnosed with uterine cancer. She, too, was given little chance for survival. Marcia did not get bitter, but instead took her trust in God to new levels. At the same time, her oldest daughter was also going through numerous health challenges. Marcia agonized during her own illness, as she knew her children needed their mother, and her husband needed his wife. Graciously, God granted her healing.

Marcia did not draw inward throughout these challenges, or hide them from others, or pretend that everything was "all good." She reached out for support and continued to graduate to new levels in the "school of trust." She made the choice to trust and to not grow bitter, even though it was a battle to surrender to God's will. Marcia exemplified the scripture in 2 Corinthians 1:3–7 and comforted others with the comfort she had received in her suffering. Knowing she was not alone in her experiences, she opened her heart, her mouth, and her home—and invited others in.

I watch Marcia as she engages other women—strong and weak—and helps them understand that "cracked vessels" have great worth. She assures them that the potter did not make a mistake as he shaped and fashioned each one of them. Many women who experience such pain retreat into themselves, for fear of experiencing further pain. Using bricks formed out of their anguish, they build walls around their hearts. But Marcia continues to tear down the fortress that attempts to form to "protect" her heart, choosing instead to allow others to walk in to see and experience her battlefield. This invitation allows other women to find strength for their own journeys. Amazingly, Marcia finds an ability to "laugh at the days to come" as she experiences real life. And when the laughter is hard to find, she knows she must be honest about that as well. She finds a way, through her friendship with God, to trust and to open wide her heart.

Recently Marcia experienced yet another heartache—every mother's worst nightmare. Her youngest son, David, then thirty-five years old, was also diagnosed with leukemia. She stood by her son, side by side with his new bride, as David suffered through rounds of chemotherapy and a stem cell transplant. While Marcia continued to speak with joy about her talented and loving son, she also spoke honestly about her fears. Friends near and far rejoiced with her when it seemed David's cancer was cured. But then the unthinkable happened. The leukemia relapsed with a vengeance, and David succumbed to the disease. While Marcia wrestled and pleaded with her God, even now she knows that God is with her, comforting her as only he can. Thousands of friends have watched and hurt and wept with her.

Because of Marcia's vulnerability, she experiences depth in her friendships and an uncanny ability to comfort those who are also afflicted. She teaches everyone who knows her to "open wide our hearts." The light of God shines brilliantly through the "cracks" in the vessel of her life—and continues to impact more souls than she can know. "But we have this treasure in jars of clay to show that this all-surpassing power is from God and not from us" (2 Corinthians 4:7).

CHAPTER FOUR

Sarah: Leadership and Courage
Robin Williams

Genesis 12-23

"We're moving!" Abram announced. "And I have no idea where we're going!" At sixty-five years old, God asked Sarai to move with her husband, Abram, to . . . somewhere. Moving is hard enough, but moving to a place that is unknown is downright scary.

What enabled Sarai (later renamed Sarah) to move without knowing where she was going? Courage. After all, how can you be courageous if you don't feel fearful? That would be like having perseverance when you don't ever want to quit! Courage is "the quality of mind or spirit that enables a person to face difficulty, danger, pain, etc., without fear."[6] Sarah's encounters with her God gave her the quality of mind and spirit she needed to be a woman of courage.

It takes courage to persevere in faith.

God waited until Abram was seventy-five years old and Sarah was sixty-five before asking them to pack their things, leave the country of their heritage, and move to a land that he would show them. The move would require living in tents. Just living in a tent would make you a courageous woman—flimsy walls, little privacy, sand everywhere . . . and who knows what kind of critters might find their way into your tent. You would have to become a tough woman to survive in those times! Sarai had been accustomed to living in a home with walls in Ur of the Chaldeans.

She had heard the stories of Adam and Noah and her great-great-great-grandfathers many times. These stories of God's love and protection had produced in her the convictions she needed to face the future. She knew that just as God had provided for her ancestors, so he would also provide for and protect her. Remembering the ways God has always provided for his people can also give us courage. Sarai's faithful, spirited thoughts may have made her look at this move as a wondrous adventure.

Can you imagine the conversations Sarai and Abram must have had? She probably had numerous objections to the move, and she may have verbalized the obstacles—but when it came time to go, she went. She put one foot in front of the other and moved away from that which she knew toward a "world unknown." Those first steps away from home took a tremendous amount of courage. When the way grew difficult along the way, her steps required "persevering courage."

We all need courage and faith just to live life as a Christian. And if we want to lead other people towards God, we will need even more courage, and even more faith. A woman's faith and trust in her husband (or the brother she leads with) are crucial in order for her leadership to be powerful. This trust is ultimately based on a woman's trust in God—not men. Sarai's respect and trust enabled her to follow her husband and not give into her fears, because she knew that God, not Abram, was in control, and was watching over her. How do you handle difficult situations and times of change? Do you want to quit when things get hard, or do you, as a courageous leader, trust in the mighty workings of God and put one foot in front of the other with each new adventure?

It takes courage to be submissive.

Over the years, Sarai would face more tests of faith, requiring her courage to increase. With much trepidation, Sarai found herself sitting in the courts of Pharaoh, surrounded by other beautiful women chosen to be his wives. Abram had asked Sarai to tell Pharaoh that she was Abram's sister. She understood that Abram had told her this to ensure his safety and spare his life, but what was going to happen to her? She was Abram's half-sister, but she was also his wife! She didn't belong there; she belonged with Abram. How could he do this to her? What was her God trying to teach her now? Was Sarai being asked to be the wife of a Pharaoh? How could she get out of this mess?

Sarai must have experienced great anxiety and fear. She had no idea how she would get out of her situation, but she did know that her God was with her. He had promised to make Abram a great nation, saying that Abram would be blessed and that his name would be great, blessing all the families of the earth. Sarai needed to recall all of God's promises in order to regain her courage to submit to Abram's lead. Her fears could have dominated her thoughts, but she chose to hold to God's promises.

As she saw Pharaoh treating Abram well, providing him with sheep, oxen, donkeys, camels and servants, her anxious heart may have started to calm. When plagues struck Pharaoh's house and the truth about Abram and Sarai's marriage came out, her fears must have returned. But God intervened, and they were told to leave—with no consequences. With thankful hearts, Sarai and Abram were reunited again. Sarai realized she could trust the One who was leading them. She had not given way to fear, and God had come through (1 Peter 3:6).

Even though we see God working and protecting us, we can still grow impatient with God's plans, as Sarai did. When she was seventy-five, Sarai decided she needed to help God fulfill his promise to give them a child. We can often be like her, thinking that God needs our intervention when we don't approve of his timing or mode of operation. So Sarai gave Abram her servant girl to conceive and carry "their" child. Sarai still needed to learn more about having courage to entrust herself to God's plan and timing.

And then again, when she was ninety years old, Abram passed Sarai off as his sister when they traveled through King Abimelech's territory. The king took her to be his wife, but God intervened and told him the truth in a dream. Again, God came to Sarai's rescue. God wanted her to totally trust him, despite Abram's lack of faith at that time. He put her in situations that would test her faith and submission. Are you courageous when you're put in situations that test your trust?

If, after we make a couple of suggestions or requests (as Sarai probably did), but our husbands (or the brothers we lead with) don't change their minds, we need the courage to submit and trust God to work through (and even in spite of) the situation. This quiet and gentle spirit is "of great worth" to God (1 Peter 3:4¬). He will protect us, and work through and in spite of our situation. He doesn't need us to take over. We need to gain the courage to entrust ourselves to the One who judges justly—just as Jesus did on the cross and as Sarai did when she was put in life-threatening situations. When we gain this courage, we give God the chance to work more powerfully.

It takes courage to laugh at things to come.

When Abram was ninety-nine years old, God appeared to him and reaffirmed his promise to him. God then changed Abram's name to Abraham, which means "father of nations," and changed Sarai's name, "princess," to Sarah, meaning "princess of many"[7]— thus confirming his promise. At that time, Abraham fell on his face and laughed. Sarah wasn't present that day to hear God repeat his promise. So when God returned a few months later in the form of men, he wanted to make sure that Sarah was present. Even though she was in the back of the tent, the Lord heard her laugh. She couldn't believe she would have the pleasure of having a child at her age. They both laughed. I love the fact that Abraham and Sarah could laugh with God. And even though they were laughing at the implausibility of God's plan in their minds, they were vulnerable with God; they were themselves. That's the kind of relationship God wants with us. Isn't it interesting that he doesn't correct their laughter; he only corrects Sarah for lying about laughing.

It takes courage to laugh, because laughing makes us vulnerable; we can look silly laughing, or we might laugh at the wrong thing. Laughter that derides someone or puts someone down is not good; but laughter that expresses faith and gratitude is a gift from God (Psalm 126:2). Laughter can give us courage when we face danger, the unknown, fear, or the impossible. Just as it did for Abraham and Sarah, laughter can help us remember that God is the only one we can turn to during those times.

Being able to laugh at the times to come during hard times demonstrates how much we are trusting God with our lives. A courageous leader can laugh at the times to come. If we take everything too seriously, we will not be as effective as we can be. Part of leadership is helping people know that God wants us to enjoy life. To do that, we need to enjoy life. Ecclesiastes 3:4 says that there is a time to laugh. Do you know when that time is?

It takes courage to be happy and at peace when we are not in control or do not know what the future may hold. Our ability to laugh and trust God with our future demonstrates courage and faith. We may not know where God is leading us, but like Sarah, we can trust that he is, in fact, leading. He knows where he is taking us, even when we do not. We may not live the life we were expecting, and God may reveal only a few steps of our journey at a time, but if we develop the kind of trust and courage and humor that Sarah had, we can find joy in the journey, wherever it leads.

- What "first steps" as a courageous leader do you need to take in order to overcome a fear of "going to an unknown place"?
- As a courageous leader, do you trust God even when others around you make decisions different than you would make?
- Do you often recount and thank God for the miracles in the Scriptures and for the times he has protected you and rescued you from trouble?
- Do you have the courage to wait on God, or do you try to "help" him along?
- Can you laugh at the days to come, knowing God is in control?
- Do you take time to laugh and enjoy all God has given you?

Let us be like Sarah, courageously putting one foot in front of the other, trusting God that he is able to lead us forward. What a turn history would have taken if Sarah had not had the courage to go. Because of her faith, we have an inspiring example to follow as we travel along our own journeys.

Encourage *means to put courage into someone. People need to hear me say, "You* are *a strong person!", "You* will *make it through this!", "God sees you and cares what you are going through." It's amazing what a little encouragement can do!*

—Chris Fuqua, Los Angeles, California

The times when I have had to be most courageous over the years have usually involved facing things I didn't want to face about myself, speaking the truth in love to someone when it was very difficult, or enduring something scary involving my kids' health or safety. I have found that praying, reciting scriptures that I have memorized previously, and even singing help me get through the scariest times.

— Karen Louis, Singapore

Courage is not the absence of fear, but means acting righteously because we are motivated by love (1 John 4:18). Courage, as leaders, often involves taking on the messy situations that others do not want to involve themselves with. Love is what motivates us to have this courage.

—Caron Vassallo, Melbourne, Australia

Fear can keep us from speaking the truth in love. Don't just "almost" say something. With sincere love and kindness, say what you mean and mean what you say.

— Jeanie Shaw, Burlington, Massachusetts

Courage is telling the story of who you are with your whole heart. It's scary, even as leaders, to be completely open and authentic because we can get caught up in what we think we should be, and how we should act—and forget the joy and freedom that comes from being real and vulnerable. We all want to feel a sense of worth and belonging. Fear of failure, shame, or feeling we don't measure up to a certain standard can keep us from being vulnerable.

—Laura Fix, Londonderry, New Hampshire

PROFILE

Corrina, Mumbai, India: Courage

by Cheryl Pereira, Mumbai, India

Corrina was baptized during the summer of 1987, a few months after the Mumbai Church of Christ began. Although she was excited about her new life, her life at home was difficult. Corrina's dad had worked in the Middle East at one time. During this time, he married another woman and had another family. He put this other family before Corrina's, and gave them much greater priority—more importance and more love. Most of the money he earned went to them. Sadly, he never paid much attention to Corrina, her brothers, or her mother. They continually struggled to make ends meet. Corrina's dad became very upset when Corrina became a disciple and left their traditional church. His main complaint was that she would have no place to be buried, as her new church did not own a burial ground.

The rest of her family was also very unhappy about Corrina's decision to become a Christian, and they opposed her intensely. In the fall after Corrina was baptized, she had to undergo open-heart surgery. Once she was discharged from the hospital, she rested for a week, and then decided she would attend a Friday devotional. When she asked one of her brothers for permission, he was so furious that he hit her, even though he was aware that she was under post-operative care.

When Jim and Mo, two of the brothers on the mission team, went to visit Corrina, her brother threatened them and tried to hit them with tube lights (tube lights are long, tube-shaped fluorescent lights, which many Indians use instead of light bulbs). He then burned Corrina's Bible and warned her that if she tried to go to church, he would beat her again. But Corrina was undaunted. She would sneak out to church when he was not around. Whenever anyone saw her in the fellowship, she was always smiling. There was no hint of the trauma she was going through at home.

One day, she waited for her brother to go out, and then left the house to come to church. On her way, she met him. He was not aware of where she was going, so he offered to drop her off on his bike. She told him she was going to church, fully expecting him to get off the bike and give her another thrashing. But instead, he just kicked the bike into gear and rode off—just like that. After that, she had no more problems, and no one in her family paid attention to where she went on Sundays. The persecution completely stopped. Many prayers were answered. It was a miracle.

After this, Corrina took a babysitting job with a Christian family so that she could have more fellowship with the disciples. Once her health improved, she found a regular job. Her health and job situation grew more stable, and she got married to one of the disciples. Unfortunately, her health problems continued, and she had two more surgeries. But even with all of her health challenges, God blessed her and her husband with four children.

As years went on, Corrina's dad grew older, and needed a lot of care. He turned to Corrina's brothers for help, but they decided to treat him in the same way he had treated them. They wouldn't even allow him to sleep in the house. He was forced to sleep outside in the rain while his health was quickly deteriorating. Realizing that he had nowhere to go, he went to Corrina's doorstep, asking her to take him in and care for him during his last days. Corrina took him in and lovingly cared for him. This was not easy, as Corrina and her husband and four children live in a tiny apartment comprised of one bedroom, a kitchen, and a bathroom. The family gave Corrina's dad the bed, while Corrina and her husband and children slept on the floor.

Nearly a year after he moved in with Corrina, her dad was baptized. The love of God expressed to him through his daughter showed him the love of Jesus. A couple of weeks later, he left this world to be with our Lord and Savior.

Corrina has been a very dear friend and a hero in the faith to many who know her in India. We love her and her family deeply. Corrina's courage has helped many to find faith in the Lord.

CHAPTER FIVE

The Sinful Woman: Leadership and Gratitude

Teresa Fontenot

Luke 7:36-50

The words and miracles of Jesus have been spreading like wildfire. He has eaten with sinners, healed a Gentile soldier's sick daughter, and even raised a widow's son from the dead! Rejoicing and excitement fill the streets. His words offer life and hope for anyone who believes them.

The woman feels hope, that long-forgotten feeling, blooming inside as she listens…gradually she comes to understand that even she can repent and be forgiven. Jesus' words reach into the brokenness of her soul and touch the overwhelming guilt she trudges through each day. His promise of freedom and acceptance refresh her. At last she sees through his eyes the ugliness of her sinful life and the promise of who she could become. And she begins to hope, to believe. Jesus has compassion on her shame. He might not know her name, but he knows her heart. The joy of it is bursting inside of her. She is *loved!* How could she love in return? What can she do to show her gratitude? It would have to be the most wonderful gift imaginable. It must be something that shows honor and respect. That's it—perfume! She will anoint him with perfume. She will pour out the scent of her old life onto his head and hands, transforming it from the aroma of death to life. She will leave this mark of her trade on Jesus, and in his presence it will become pure and heavenly. It is a great idea. Now she needs a plan to carry it out.

Extravagant gratitude

Jesus is having dinner at the house of Simon, a Pharisee, that evening. She had been hoping for a less conspicuous (and possibly hostile) setting, but she might never have another chance. The guests are dining out in the courtyard in the cool of the evening. The street gives her easy access, and she slips in unnoticed to stand at Jesus' feet as the guests recline. Aware of the stares and scowls from the dinner guests as they catch sight of her, she says nothing. She knows that Jesus accepts sinners. All she wants is to pour perfume on his head to recognize him as Lord, and to express her gratitude. But what is this? As she is standing by his feet, she can see that they are dirty. No one has washed Jesus' feet! They are not treating him as the Lord. They are insulting him! How could they? Indignation and compassion well up inside her and the tears begin to pour from her like rain. She can't ask for water and she has no towel, but her tears are enough to wash his feet. Her dress could be used for drying, but no, she will let down her hair. She must give something of her *self* to him, expressing the intimacy and loyalty she feels. Completely unaware of anyone but Jesus, she wipes, cleanses and kisses his feet. It is so wonderful to serve him, to touch him and to love him. This is a heavenly moment for her.

From shame to peace

As Jesus relates a parable to Simon, she realizes there is a lesson for each of them in it. Understanding clearly that she has the greater debt, she is very comfortable with an extreme outpouring of love. Simon, on the other hand, never seems to "connect the dots." To her it is a simple point: There is a direct correlation between forgiveness and love. It seems so obvious. Having the debt of your sins canceled—what could be more extraordinary than that? She is the only one at the dinner party who understands that this man, called Jesus, can forgive sins. And that very faith will save her. This unnamed woman does truly "go in peace," forever changed.

The perspective of gratitude

Gratitude changes everything. When we can see the good as well as the bad in a situation, we find freedom and joy. We can't stay stuck when we are grateful. Gratitude gives us a new future. This woman couldn't change her past, but the new inner life that Jesus promised her could forever alter her future. She was aggressively grateful. Nothing could stop her from letting Jesus know the difference he was making in her life. The fact that others were present to witness her response to forgiveness was just part of God's plan. She served as the visual aid for one of Jesus' most important lessons. The formula is simple: Much forgiveness=much love.

Too bad Simon didn't need much forgiveness in his life. Simon was stuck. Before we fall into Simon's trap of judging, we must admit that we all get stuck at times. We are lacking in gratitude and love. We know we are sinners, and therefore need forgiveness, but sometimes we just can't see our sin specifically. We have a general understanding, but no concrete examples come to mind. We have become dull.

The fact is, we are still BIG sinners. We have just become good at hiding our sins, even from ourselves. The God of full disclosure will shine his brightness into our hearts, exposing us…if we want it. We only have to ask.

Don't forget that finding gratitude begins with brokenness over sin. The pain of the cross brings the joy of the resurrection.

None of us are naturally grateful. Gratitude is something we must practice if we want to become good at it. We are such consumer-driven people, always striving to attain, that we fail to consider and appreciate what we have been given. Gratitude is more than a feeling. It is meant to be expressed. Jesus expected it from Simon, from the nine lepers that didn't return (Luke 17:11–19), and he expects it from us.

Humility and gratitude go hand in hand. We must admit that we are not self-sufficient in order to express the debt we owe to God and others. A humble heart is a grateful heart, just as an ungrateful heart is filled with pride. God gave us the perfect picture of this in this account of Simon and the "sinful" woman.

As leaders, our love will decrease and wane if we lose sight of our indebtedness. It is all too easy to end up in Simon's shoes. As we mature in our walk with Jesus, our gratitude should only increase. The enormity of what we owe to Jesus should become more obvious as we grow in our faith. The day of our baptism was not the high point of our gratitude—it was only the beginning!

An attitude of gratitude:

"Entitlement and self-absorption are massive impediments to gratitude. You will certainly not feel grateful when you do receive what you think you have coming, because after all, you have it coming. Counting blessings will be ineffective because grievances will always outnumber gifts."

—Dr. Robert Emmons, a well-known researcher on gratitude[8]

Jesus, our example of leadership, taught this important principle in Luke 17:7–10:

"Suppose one of you had a servant plowing or looking after the sheep. Would he say to the servant when he comes in from the field, 'Come along now and sit down to eat'? Would he not rather say, 'Prepare my supper, get yourself ready and wait on me while I eat and drink; after that you may eat and drink'? Would he thank the servant because he did what he was told to do? So you also, when you have done everything you were told to do, should say, 'We are unworthy servants; we have only done our duty.'"

The truth is, everything God has done for us, especially offering forgiveness, is a gift, and we should live our lives with that in mind. If we lead, it should be with a heart of gratitude, an attitude that "this is the least I can do for the God who has given me everything." But sometimes we lose that perspective. We begin to fight God with our thoughts, even as outwardly we practice servant leadership; we can start to feel that we deserve a break, or recognition, or thanks. While we do need to honor and appreciate each other, a grateful leader will continue to give and serve because of her understanding of what God has done for her—her service is not dependent upon ever receiving recognition for her labors.

As you follow Christ and as you strive to lead others in his ways, let your every action come from a place of gratitude, not duty. When the mantle of leadership begins to feel heavy, remember the "sinful woman" and your own sinful days—all that Jesus has saved you from. Remember *why* you do what you do, and never forget the One for whom you do it.

- Do you struggle with feeling entitled, overlooked, or unappreciated? How does this affect your love for God and others? How can you change your perspective?
- Are you in the habit of saying "thank you" and noticing what other people do to serve?
- Have you become dull in your relationship with God? What steps can you take to increase your love?
- Begin keeping a daily journal, reminding yourself of all the blessings you have been given. The list is never-ending, as we serve the great God of generosity!

The sinful woman reminds us of who we are before God, and the gratitude that should flow from the depths of our souls.

I think the command to "give thanks always" (1 Thessalonians 5:18) may be the most disobeyed command in the Bible. It seems easier to find something to complain about than to be grateful. Giving thanks is one of the quickest ways to help fight temptations.

—Gloria Baird, Los Angeles, California

Gratitude toward God and toward people changes one's entire perspective on life. This is a helpful truth to keep in mind by the hour! I have learned that I need not only to feel grateful, but to express my gratitude to people frequently. Everyone needs a steady dose of encouragement and appreciation.

— Mary Lou Craig, Boonton, New Jersey

If Paul can be grateful while in a dark dungeon prison while writing Philippians, surely I can be grateful every day for both the wonderful blessings and hard times in my life which help me to grow. It is so important for me to take every opportunity to be grateful for those who are around me and to express my gratitude to them.

—Sally Hooper, Dallas, Texas

Practicing gratitude is one of the greatest weapons we have against Satan. The daily practice of gratitude protects our hearts.

—Virginia Lefler, Chicago, Illinois

The daily, small pleasures that God provides for us should give us joy:
- *a tasty home-cooked meal*
- *buying a special gift for our child*
- *watching a sunset with a loved one*
- *an answered prayer, no matter how small*
- *a smile for us from a child*

If we are truly thankful to God for our lives, then we cannot help but share that joy with others.

—Caron Vassillo, Melbourne, Australia

PROFILE

Mealea Tan, Cambodia: Gratitude
by Erica Kim, Colorado

"Pol Pot's army killed every member of my family. I have no one left," said Mealea Tan as her husband, Dr. Kim Meng Tan, held her hand. Tears streamed down her face as she recounted this tragic episode of her life.

Sadly, Mealea is just one of many Cambodians who lost their entire family during the genocide that ravaged their country from 1975 to 1979. It is estimated that more than two million Cambodians were killed—or about twenty percent of the total population.

Cambodia was known as the "Pearl of the Orient" until the early seventies. Unknown to the Western world until the mid- to late eighties, Cambodia's leader, Pol Pot, and his army, known as the Khmer Rouge (or to the Cambodians as **Angkar**), had successfully taken most of the political leaders and their families, as well as most of the doctors, educators, and businessmen, to be tortured and killed in one of the bloodiest genocides in modern history.

Much like the Nazi concentration camps, families were separated by sexes and age, then forced to do hard labor in the fields with little food under extremely unsanitary conditions. The children were forced to sleep in small areas, where they were lined up like the slaves on the nineteenth-century slave ships—alternating head to toe on the floor. They were given small pots to relieve themselves in, but were not allowed to leave the room. The lack of baths caused their hair to be matted and filled with lice.

Mealea recounted her experience during this time and said: "I was a very young girl, eight years old, during the Pol Pot regime. My younger brother and I were with my grandparents. My parents had been in another province called *Siem Reap*, having been drafted for military duty. I lived with a group of children who were the same age. They gave us limited food—three to four spoons of rice per meal, only two meals a day. They made us work very, very hard every day with no weekend or rest for almost four years. We slept in camps that were wet with urine and stool. We had lice all over our head and skin. The hardest part was that my whole family—my parents, one sister and two brothers—were all killed by the Pol Pot regime." As she said these words, tears kept flooding out of her eyes, leaving her almost unable to converse.

"I'm sorry, I'm sorry," she apologized as she spoke. "It's just so hard for me to remember and talk about the most painful part of my life. I want to forget it all." Then she added, "The Khmer Rouge starved my little brother to death. He was only five years old. I miss him."

Obviously, a country that undergoes such trauma is left with incalculable needs, particularly with the top leaders of the country all dead or deported to other countries. So many people are left heartbroken and hopeless. But God provided hope for Mealea and many others through the arrival of several missionaries in 1992. For Mealea, meeting those missionaries was the beginning of hope in her life. Her bitterness was transformed into joy as she and her husband made Jesus their Lord and were baptized.

Though Pol Pot killed Mealea's entire family through unbearable torture, there is no longer any bitterness and anger in her heart. She has been able to let go of her fear and loneliness as well. God has given her a new family in Christ with her husband at her side. Her husband, Dr. Kim Meng Tan, serves in HOPE *worldwide's* hospital in Phnom Penh, where he delivers medical care and plays a key role in training up new Cambodian doctors.

Mealea has two teenage daughters who are both Christians. Her son is attending HOPE *worldwide's* Goldstone School. Her life has been blessed spiritually, emotionally, and physically, in more ways than she can count. Now she says, "I thank God every day because I cannot believe how blessed I am right now. I can't imagine where my life would be at right now without him!"

CHAPTER SIX

The Bleeding Woman: Leadership and Faith

Jeanie Shaw

Mark 5:21-34; Luke 8:40-48

An important man had garnered Jesus' attention. Together, he and Jesus appeared to be in a hurry. A large crowd had gathered and was following Jesus and this man. The word buzzing through the crowd was that the synagogue leader, Jairus, had pleaded for Jesus to go to his house to heal his daughter, who was gravely ill. It seemed they were on the way to his house.

A woman saw and heard the commotion, and quickly took it in. Jesus had drawn a crowd, yet was responding to a man's passionate plea. The man was saying something about the touch of Jesus—if only Jesus could touch his daughter she could be well. The woman was trying to make sense of this scene unfolding before her eyes. She felt fear, desperation, and amazement all at once. She had been on her menstrual period every single day for twelve years, often hemorrhaging. Though she had seen many doctors and spent all her money, no one could help her. Instead of getting better, the bleeding got worse and worse. She was anemic, tired, and in great physical and emotional pain. Her situation was so severe that she could not conceal it. She would often bleed through her clothing and could not hide the stench of the blood. This "private" ailment was not really private. She was known in her community as the "bleeding woman." In her mind, she may as well have been called "the woman who smelled" or the "woman with oozing sores in her private parts." Over the years, she had lost her sense of value and purpose. She felt forgotten by God. The doctors had no answers for her.

But somehow, with what she had seen and heard from the crowd, she knew Jesus could heal her. She did not hesitate to move forward—she simply had to get to Jesus. She went with what appeared to others as a reckless abandon. To her this move was not reckless, but urgent. She was absolutely convinced that Jesus had the power to heal her that others did not have. She would not be deterred.

Jesus was with an "important" man who was on a mission. What possessed this unknown, humiliated, and sickly woman to push her way through the crowd in order to touch the hem of Jesus' garment? So many things could have kept her from reaching for Jesus: hesitation, doubt, fear, a feeling of insignificance, her lack of a plan. Any one of these obstacles could have held her back.

She lacked money, health, and status—but she did not lack faith. As she fell to her knees, she was able to see the fabric of Jesus' garment flow behind him. Her heart raced as she finally felt the texture of the fabric on her fingertips. She had reached Jesus! Was it her imagination, or did the bleeding she had lived with for so long suddenly stop? Yes, it was true—she knew she had stopped bleeding!

Suddenly Jesus interrupted his mission for Jairus and his daughter, turned around to the crowd and asked, "Who touched me?" The disciples were somewhat befuddled by his question since people all around him had been brushing up against him. What was he talking about? Dozens of people were touching him! But clearly something—some*one*—had gotten Jesus' attention. Just as the woman felt healing inside of her body, Jesus felt power go out of his body.

The no-longer-bleeding woman heard Jesus' question loud and clear. What had she done? This was her chance to slip away, to shrink back in the crowd unnoticed, and escape as fast as possible. And yet she understood that Jesus was not someone to hide from—and she knew he knew she had just been healed. Although she could have run in the other direction, she ran toward Jesus . . . once again falling to her knees. She could not ignore or deny what had happened, no matter what the cost (perhaps even the punishment) might be for her. Trembling, she said to him (and the whole crowd), "It was me."

She explained why she had touched him and how with a single touch she had been healed. The reason why she did this was not that complicated. She believed Jesus could heal her, she wanted to get well, and she needed to contact his power. Not only did she contact his power, but she also came in contact with his love. Jesus' response to her was, "Daughter, your faith has healed you. Go in peace and be freed from your suffering" (Mark 5:34). The word *daughter* rang in her ears like a beautiful song. Jesus had interrupted his journey to consider her, to call her *daughter*, to free her from her suffering and to send her off with his blessing.

Although this woman may have seemed insignificant in comparison to Jairus, the synagogue ruler, Jesus valued her and stopped the crowd to reward her faith. Even today, her faith inspires. Faith is foundational to spiritual leadership.

What qualities of faith can we imitate and learn from the "no-longer-bleeding woman"?

- **Faith is contagious.** Perhaps this woman had observed Jairus' faith as he persuaded Jesus to act on behalf of his daughter. She may have thought, *If Jairus believes this, why can't I?* Or perhaps she had already heard of Jesus' teaching and actions, and had come to believe that Jesus' promises were real and were for her. Either way, faith begets faith. Just as we sometimes need to "borrow" someone else's faith, so our faith can have a great ripple effect on others who see our faith in action.

- **Faith steps forward in spite of the facts.** The bleeding woman had spent a dozen years and all of her money looking for a cure. The doctors simply could not help her. Something was broken, and according to the facts on hand, it was not fixable. This woman believed that Jesus possessed something outside the rules of science and biology—outside human reason and ability. Had she not believed, she would not have stepped forward to put herself in the midst of a crowd—she wouldn't have risked setting herself up for further disappointment and embarrassment. Spiritual leadership steps forward—toward Jesus—even when doing so makes no sense on a human level.

- **Faith doesn't care what others think.** How easy it is to be swayed by what others think of us. The bleeding woman could have been self-conscious. She could have allowed her faith to be squelched by the fear of how she would look to others. Why risk exposing her weakness and illness to a crowd? When we care too much about how we are viewed, we can miss out on the promises God has in store for us.

- **Faith often approaches Jesus on our knees.** The bleeding woman touched the hem of Jesus' garment. She would have needed to be on her knees or bowing low in order to do this. And moments later, when Jesus inquired of the crowd, she ran toward him and fell on her knees before him. Through faith we know we are unworthy of Jesus' blessings, and yet we feel the confidence to come before him to ask for grace and mercy. Spiritual leaders most often find faith on their knees—or in a posture before God that expresses our dependence on his grace, mercy, and power.

- **Faith gets Jesus' attention.** Numerous scriptures show Jesus noticing and admiring an individual's faith. Faith moves him. The bleeding woman believed that Jesus cared for her and was somehow not too busy to give her attention. She dared to push through the crowd to reach Jesus, to touch him and get his attention.

- **Faith dares to imagine.** While the bleeding woman could have easily resigned herself to a lifetime of bleeding, she dared to imagine that life could be different. She dreamed of a breakthrough that could be life-changing. Spiritual leadership keeps dreaming of breakthroughs, not held back by the way things currently are.

- **Faith transfers the power of God to our life.** Perhaps the bleeding woman remembered that God had spoken the world into existence, saved Noah through the flood, helped the Israelites cross the Jordan on dry land, made the sun stand still, closed the mouths of lions, protected God's men from burning in a fiery furnace, and sent his Son into her world to perform miracles and show his love. All this was power beyond her imagination. Her faith in the power of God, revealed and displayed in his Son, meant that she could receive life-changing power. Spiritual leadership believes that God's power is available for us, and will flow directly from him to us.

- **Faith speaks up.** The bleeding woman's faith not only got Jesus' attention, but also the attention of a huge crowd. Although she came to Jesus trembling, she still spoke up and took responsibility for her faith. Spiritual leadership is willing speak up for our faith. We may be trembling, as she was, but she "owned up" to her faith.

- **Faith believes that God loves us.** This woman's faith trusted that Jesus would care about her. Her faith resulted in her being called "daughter" by Jesus. Jesus didn't say to her, "Bleeding woman, your faith has healed you! Go in peace." He called her *daughter* and gave her the desire of her heart. True faith believes God when he tells us that we are loved as daughters, and believes when he tells us that he is out for our good. Faith believes, no matter the outcome, that God will give us what we need—even if it is not what we want.

- Think of a time when your faith grew from observing another person's faith. How might your faith inspire someone else?

- How might you take a "first step" of faith in an area where you doubt yourself, or with something that seems impossible?

- In what situations are you most tempted to let other people's opinions keep you from acting in faith?

- Is it easy for you to assume you could not really get Jesus' attention, or do you keep pushing through in prayer until you "touch" him? How can you grow in faith so that Jesus can't help but notice the depth of your desire for his attention toward a particular situation?

- Where do you feel stuck? In school? In your career? In your spiritual walk? In your family life? Do you imagine what things could look like in your life with a breakthrough? Do you take your requests to God in faith?

Just as the bleeding woman followed her faith to reach the power of God, let us also have faith that goes beyond what we have so far dared to ask or imagine.

I have prayed to be a woman of great faith—and then I cringe when I realize that the times that test my faith the most are the times I face things I didn't ask for, don't understand, don't like, and don't want! Where fear comes in, faith goes out—but where faith comes in, fear goes out!

—Gloria Baird, Los Angeles, California

Others must see me trusting God in the midst of trials or seemingly impossible situations. I must be open and vulnerable with my life and share not only the victories, but my struggles as well.

—Sally Hooper, Dallas, Texas

Possessing a confident, resilient faith that others can see is crucial for leaders— otherwise they cannot imitate our faith. Romans 4:18 tells us that God can make something from nothing. Sometimes weaker disciples may need to borrow our faith for a while.

—Caron Vassallo, Melbourne, Australia

Don't coast when it comes to building your faith. It is one of your most treasured qualities as a Christian and as a leader. It is the foundation of your relationship with God. Whatever builds your faith, make sure you are taking the time to do so.

—Virginia Lefler, Chicago, Illinois

The strongest rebukes from Jesus to his disciples were given for their lack of faith. Train yourself to trust in what God can see but we cannot. Remember that it is faith in God, not faith in faith, that builds true faith—and remember to lead from faith. "The only thing that counts is faith expressing itself through love" (Galatians 5:6).

—Teresa Fontenot, Sydney, Australia

Not too long after our little Singapore mission team was sent out, I discovered that the sister who was supposed to come and lead the women wasn't coming, and that this responsibility would be given to me. What a shock! All I could do was to rely on the word of God and believe what I was reading. I knew full well I would have to have faith that God could work through me, because I knew I couldn't do anything on my own. My faith grew, and I kept reading and believing. Faith had to be my foundation from the day I arrived in Singapore twenty-six years ago.

—Karen Louis, Singapore

PROFILE

Ana Morrell, Edinburgh, Scotland: Faith

by Nadine Templer, New Delhi, India

Ana Morrell became a disciple more than twenty years ago in London. At the time, she had been married for three years. As she changed her life, her husband watched her faith grow. Ana is known for her faith, warmth, and hospitality. She is also one of the most evangelistic people I have met, always sharing her faith. I have been encouraged by her constant smile.

Ana prayed consistently for her husband. He would occasionally attend church, and even studied the Bible a few times. He was always friendly to the members of the church, but was never really interested in becoming a disciple. A few years ago, he found out he had developed cancer. His wife desperately wanted him to find a relationship with God.

Ana was true to her faith, even though things were very hard. She never wavered, and six days before he passed away David was baptized! Here Ana shares some of the convictions she gained along the way:

> My faith comes from taking God at his word, deciding to believe what the Bible says, and keeping that in my head, whether or not things are going well. I feel that God always gives me reasons to believe and steps to take. When I decide to walk according to the Scriptures, God never lets me down. So when David got sick, I decided to believe that God was in control. I had to surrender and decide to stay faithful even if he died without being baptized. It was extremely difficult, but God always encouraged me through the people around me. I decided I would not give up until I saw my husband buried.
>
> I now realize that God is among us all the time, doing miracles every day, whether we see them or not—from the littlest things, to things that are completely out of our control. We just need to take each step believing in his words and not believing what Satan tries

to tell us. I'm still amazed that David was baptized six days before he died—after nearly twenty-three years of resisting God.

I am grateful, not because of my righteousness, but because God loved him. David decided to listen to God, and God spared me further heartbreak. I take each day as it comes—filled with gratitude while looking to God. As I said before, God has never let me down yet, and I know he never will. My part is to believe his words and take him at his word—one step at a time—and do my best to walk every day with him.

I need this faith for my loved ones who are yet to be saved, as well as for enduring the struggles that come from losing my husband. God is still God, and there is always hope because of the cross.

I hope this helps anyone who is struggling. The battle has been won and God is always faithful. We just need to remember that.

Ben Brady is the evangelist of the church in Edinburgh, Scotland, where Ana now lives. He studied the Bible with Ana's husband, and he has these words to say about Ana:

> I know Ana has been a part of God's kingdom for many years, but I really only know her from our time together in the Edinburgh Church. From our arrival until now, she has offered us her love and service—and has taught me many times that with God as number one, much can be overcome.
>
> God has developed within her wisdom and peace that encourage and inspire all that know her.
>
> I became a very close part of her life during her husband's battle with cancer. He lost that battle—but gained salvation! This was a time I will never forget.
>
> Ana was lovingly persistent throughout, constantly at his bedside as he deteriorated, offering him her unconditional love while expressing her desire for him to find God in his last days. The love between them was so evident, and the pain she felt as he slipped away was obvious. Throughout this time, her faith enabled her to remain amazingly strong.
>
> She smiled broadly on the day of his baptism, as if the twenty-three years of his resistance had melted away—her faith rewarded.
>
> The Edinburgh Church and I learned vital lessons about God's faithfulness and our response to him throughout this time.

Ana's challenges have been many, but she has always come through with dignity and faith. I am blessed to be part of a church where she is a constant support to me and my family, despite those challenges. She is both an upward call (having a friend at church almost weekly), and an ever-present encouragement, serving happily in many roles.

I love and appreciate Ana, and am personally convicted and inspired by her faith.

I pray you find encouragement through Ana's faithful example. Ana's life shows us that it is never too late for God to work. He hears our prayers, he honors our faith, and he is the God of the impossible.

CHAPTER SEVEN

The Women in the Upper Room: Leadership and Prayer

Jeanie Shaw

Acts 1:9-14

They had been with Jesus. They were there when he taught the multitudes, and they were there when he taught individuals. They saw him heal people. They knew he cared about people, and they knew he cared about each one of them. They realized that Jesus treated them differently than other men did—with Jesus, they were always valued and treated with the utmost love and respect. They trusted him, and they knew without doubt that he was the Son of God. They were there when he was crucified, and afterwards, they mourned at his tomb.

And then they witnessed how, in an act beyond human comprehension, Jesus came back to life, left the tomb, and spent forty days on earth. Then suddenly, all too soon, he left—ascending into heaven. They wept, they rejoiced, and then they cried some more. Now it was time to go home.

They spent the entire day walking from the Mount of Olives back to Jerusalem—dazed and somewhat mystified. Confused. Lost. Upon their arrival in Jerusalem, these women, along with the apostles and Jesus' mother and brothers, slowly climbed the stairs to the room where they were staying. What would they do now? Their leader, their Messiah, their brother, their friend was really gone this time. Before he left, he had said something to them about waiting in Jerusalem for some unknown thing to happen—and he told them that they would be his witnesses all over the earth. They spoke to each other about the possible meaning of Jesus' parting commands, promises, and instructions. Jesus' plan must have seemed unclear, if not preposterous, to the group. They tried to get their heads and hearts around what they had heard, and wondered if perhaps they had misunderstood Jesus.

One thing was clear. Jesus had left them—*poof!*—and ascended into the clouds. The apostles had simply stood there gazing up at the clouds, perhaps hoping that there would be some writing in the sky or some further instructions from Jesus. They probably would have stayed there waiting for a long time, had not two angels asked them why they were staring at the clouds. And now, this ragtag group of disciples (made up of men and women) was together under one roof. I wonder if they remembered scriptures such as 2 Chronicles 20:12–13:

> "O our God, will you not judge them? For we have no power to face this vast army that is attacking us. We do not know what to do, but our eyes are upon you."
>
> All the men of Judah, with their wives and children and little ones, stood there before the LORD.

Certainly, the women in the upper room did not know what to do, but fortunately, their eyes were upon God.

Spiritual leaders pray when they don't know what to do.

What did these women do when they didn't know what to do? They prayed. There in that upper room they prayed, and then they prayed some more.

Their example teaches us wonderful lessons about spirituality and about leadership. When you are not sure what to do next, where do you go? Do you fret, or complain that you don't know what to do? Do you talk to everyone else about your dilemma without first approaching God? Too often we (and I count myself as chief among that *we*) want a clear plan that describes all the detailed steps we need to take and the order in which we need to take them. However, life throws us curveballs, and there will be many times when we won't know the best next step to take. Like the women in the upper room, there is no better way for us to proceed than to gather with others and approach God's throne of grace. But I have found that most people come together and *discuss* things instead of praying…perhaps we have grand intentions of praying together, but in reality, we spend most of the time talking.

Spiritual leaders gather others around themselves to pray.

While God wants us to pray on all occasions with every kind of prayer (Ephesians 6:18), there is something very powerful that happens when people come together to pray. Perhaps the women in the upper room recounted Jesus' promise in Matthew 18:19–20 that whenever two or more are gathered in his name, he is there with them—and that united prayer is powerful. Perhaps they also remembered the example of Esther, who pulled the women in around her to fast and pray when she was afraid and needed God to hear her request.

We see other examples in the book of Acts of women gathering to pray:

> On the Sabbath we went outside the city gate to the river, where we expected to find a place of prayer. We sat down and began to speak to the women who had gathered there. (Acts 16:13)

There are more than thirty references to prayer in the book of Acts, and most of them refer to disciples joined together to pray.

When we ask others to join with us in prayer, we show leadership by pointing them to God. There is no more powerful way to lead than by bringing people to our all-powerful God. Do you pray when you study the Bible with someone? Do you pray when you are together having discipleship times? When you are with others discussing a problem—perhaps a family issue or a financial issue—in the midst of your discussion, do you stop and pray together about the problem? The women in the upper room gathered to pray about their situation. In fact, Acts 1:14 tells us that this was something that all the disciples, both men and women, did constantly.

Do you pray with your children before school? Do you pray around the dinner table? Do you pray with your husband or roommates? Do you pray together with your family group about each other's needs, each other's children, and each other's spiritual growth? When you visit someone who is sick, do you pray with them? When you are "stuck" in conversation with someone (even on the phone), do you think to pray? It's easy to want to share good news with friends about our children or about accomplishments. Do we pray with others "just" to praise and thank our God for the good things he has done?

When first-century disciples gathered together, they praised God, they prayed for their leaders, they prayed for help in times of crisis, they petitioned on behalf of sinners to repent, they prayed for missions, and they asked for physical safety and healing. The women in the upper room gathered to pray. Their prayer life is still an example to us today.

Spiritual leaders expect God to work in ways beyond their understanding.

When we, like the women in the upper room, gather to pray, the impact will be felt far and wide—because God hears our prayers and God is all-powerful. Spiritual leaders turn to God and ask him to work. Spiritual leaders know God can do more than they imagine. When Esther gathered women around her to pray, the Jewish nation was saved. When the women in the upper room prayed, as was their custom, God worked in mighty ways.

No matter what our gifts or responsibilities or abilities, we can *all* gather other women together to pray. One of the greatest things we can do in life is simply take others with us to God—praising him, casting our burdens on him, confessing our sins to him, thanking him, asking him to work on others' behalf and on our own behalf, and praying for wisdom. The ripple effect of those prayers will be immeasurable. Even if we lack transportation or physical strength, we can gather friends who live close by, or we can call people on the phone—and pray. Just as power lines can cover thousands of miles, transmitting high voltage to light our rooms and heat our homes, so our prayers can impact people that live on other continents, and make a difference in the lives of people we have never even met.

- What can you implement to remind you to pray first when you "don't know what to do"?
- Who can you decide to pray together with for a united purpose?
- What are some requests you can take to God that are "more than you dare ask or imagine"?
- How can you incorporate more prayer together within the walls of your home?
- What are some ways united prayer could affect the lives of many people?

Like the women of the upper room, let us constantly and consistently go to God in prayer. These prayers can make immeasurable differences in hundreds and thousands of lives.

We may think of prayer as a means to maintain our walk with God, but it is much more than that. God has chosen to work through our prayers of faith. It is through our prayers that we unleash God's awesome power.

— Virginia Lefler, Chicago, Illinois

Coming from a non-religious background, I had no idea how to pray when I was a young Christian. I read book after book on prayer. My favorites are from classic Christian writers such as Andrew Murray and E.M. Bounds. J.I. Packer's book "Knowing God" helped me to understand better the one to whom I was praying. Becky Tirabassi's book and prayer journal helped me to be more consistent and to see my time with God as a daily appointment with the Creator of the Universe. Hannah Hurnard's "Hinds' Feet on High Places" brought me to a more surrendered place with God, and Richard Foster's writings taught me about meditating and visualizing.

— Karen Louis, Singapore

Make sure prayer is not just a habit, but a true communication with your creator. Pray before everything—relying on God's spirit to work. Pray with others so they will learn to pray.

—Jeanie Shaw, Burlington, Massachusetts

The last few years have taught me to pray. Pray about everything. Pray a lot. Pray often. Pray for other people. Ask them what you can pray for them.

—Elexa Liu, Hong Kong, China

PROFILE

Lena Johnson, London, England: Prayer

by Linda Brumley, California

Lena Johnson grew up in her grandmother's house in Ghana. Her exposure to faith was a mixture of Christianity and superstition. Although she was not a Bible reader, she was a believer in its Author, and she prayed conscientiously.

Prayer came naturally to Lena because many circumstances of her life were difficult and she often had nowhere to turn but God. She learned very early in her life to seek God as the only dependable refuge.

When she was seventeen, she moved to London to live with her mother and stepfather. Every aspect of her life changed abruptly in this new environment. Diplomats and ambassadors were frequent visitors in her parents' home, and every day she watched limos pull up in front of the house to deposit some dignitary for a meeting with her stepfather. There were many emotional adjustments to be made in this new world.

During her time away from her parents, they had converted to Islam. They pressured her to join them in this new devotion and set up appointments for her to meet with a Muslim teacher. Lena wanted to honor her parents but had reservations about exploring this unfamiliar religion. She turned to God in prayer, asking that his will be done. When the teacher failed three times to keep appointments with her for studies, Lena went to her parents and asked them to set up no more meetings. She said she had prayed for God's will to be done, and she took the teacher's failure to make the appointments as a sign from God that the Muslim faith was not his plan for her.

She was young and beautiful and ready to be loved, but naive and vulnerable. Handsome, charismatic men, rising stars in the diplomatic corps of various countries, wooed her and won her attention. By the time she was in her mid-twenties, she was a single mom with two beautiful sons. In time she married a professional man with whom she had one more son, and they moved to the United States.

But life was difficult. She steadfastly clung to her belief in God and turned to him with every hardship . . . and there were many. Prayer was a daily dependent, trusting conversation with God. She believed deeply that God heard her, cared for her, and answered her unfailingly. God-reliance was her way of life.

After a few years Lena's marriage failed, and she only had her youngest son at home. Her oldest son lived in New York and her middle son was living in Los Angeles. Her son in New York encouraged her to attend the Seattle Church of Christ. Lena's son in New York was a dancer and had met disciples at auditions. He began studying the Bible with them and was baptized. When he called Lena to encourage her to check out the church he said, "Mom, I've found the church like the one you told us was in the Bible."

In 1997, Lena visited a Sunday service with her youngest son in tow. She also brought along her middle son (who was visiting from L.A.) and his girlfriend. When I introduced myself to Lena, she immediately invited me to come to her home the next evening to study the Bible with her. When I arrived, I found that her sons and the girlfriend were there, too, and that Lena expected it to be a group Bible study. She said, "We all need to learn."

It was a strange beginning, but right away, Bible studies were set up for each of them with appropriate teachers. Lena and her oldest son had led four open hearts to seek God.

As I studied with Lena, I found her faith and prayer life challenging and inspiring. I learned as much from her as she did from me. Nothing in her life was easy—money was scarce, her health fragile, her job taxing, her schedule demanding, and her future uncertain. None of this seemed to bother Lena. She completely trusted God. Like no one else I had ever met, when Lena prayed, she left her burdens with God and trusted him. She didn't expect him to make her path smooth or to answer her requests as she made them. She believed that even in trials God had a plan, and she was eager to learn any lessons he had for her or her children. She exuded (and still exudes) calmness and contentment.

In spite of her own circumstances, Lena was exceptionally generous when she saw others in need. She brought people meals, groceries, and assistance. She served constantly and unselfishly. She learned to counsel others with deep wisdom as she coupled her growing knowledge of God's word with her hard-won wisdom from life. She began leading a women's Bible study and was sought after for her insightful counsel.

One day when I asked how she was doing, she refused to tell me. She said, "I'm not going to tell you anymore because you worry about me and worry is a sin."

Even while standing firm with this kind of conviction, Lena was a completely humble student of the Bible. God's word was relatively new to her in terms of making personal application, but she embraced it with an unquestioning faith.

Lena is back in London now, taking care of her elderly parents. Life has only gotten increasingly challenging for her. She does not know when (or if) she will be able to return to the United States, or when she might find some financial relief, or whether her health will allow her to live without pain. But Lena finds her joy in the Lord and in every life lesson he has planned for her. Her example is a constant inspiration to me, as I pray it will be for all who read her story.

Leadership

and

Competence

CHAPTER EIGHT

The Samaritan Woman: Leadership and Self-Awareness

Jeanie Shaw

John 4:1-42

She carried the empty jar on her head as she headed toward the well. She had chosen to visit during the hottest part of the day, when others would not be there, so that she would not have to endure the disapproving glares she had come to expect. She knew how she was viewed, and she knew why.

As she arrived at the well, she thought she heard someone speaking to her. Perhaps she was overheated and this was a mirage—as the only person she could see was a Jewish man. A Jewish man would certainly never speak to a woman from Samaria! She was shocked when she realized this man actually was talking to her—requesting water for his jar. Why would he be asking her? Did he not know who she was? Was he not capable of drawing water himself? Not only was she the "wrong" gender and ethnicity, but she could not even keep a husband. She could not imagine what was he thinking or why he wished to speak with her.

She could have ignored his words and slipped away, but curiosity got the best of her— how would she know why he had spoken to her unless she asked? She was not afraid to question what she did not understand. As Jesus engaged her in conversation, his request surprised her— "Go get your husband."

Without missing a beat, the woman told this man that she did not have a husband. Jesus agreed, and proceeded to tell her what he knew (which was everything) about her life—her five failed marriages and her current live-in lover. She was all too aware of these details. She knew she had messed up a lot, but as they continued to talk, Jesus convinced her she was valuable enough to have a conversation with him—and she soon found out that he was the promised Messiah.

As a result of the life change that this conversation wrought, this woman became the impetus for the spreading of the news of Jesus throughout her entire home country of Samaria— and we still learn spiritual lessons from her today. One of the qualities she possessed was self-awareness. Without self-awareness, we have many "blind spots" that impede our life and our leadership. When we are not self-aware, personal temptations and obstacles are difficult, if not impossible, to overcome. It is hard to change what we cannot see in ourselves—and this keeps us from being effective in serving others. What character attributes helped this Samaritan woman to be self-aware?

She was not afraid of truth.

This woman knew who she was and did not try to hide it. Her awareness of how she was viewed and her current state of affairs had probably humbled her and opened her heart to hear what Jesus had to say. It would have been easy for her shame to prevent her from being open with who she really was—after all, Jesus might not talk to her if he really knew her. But because she chose not to hide or run away from the truth about her life, she was not resistant to his request and observations—and to his amazing offer of living water.

What if she had not been self-aware? If she had not been honest (with herself and with Jesus) about her current situation, she would not have recognized the value Jesus saw in her and likely would have ignored his words—she would have just wanted to get away. If she had deceived herself in order to justify her way of life, she probably would have also tried to deceive Jesus when he asked her to get her husband. If she had been content to stay in her situation, she would not have asked questions of Jesus. She could have taken Jesus' request—"go get your husband"—as an accusation, and immediately resorted to a default, defensive response such as, *My life situation is not my fault; you don't understand me; you are judging me; my life is none of your business; of course I know what living water is—and I don't need any of your water.*

Instead, she accepted his accurate account of her life. Hearing truthful input from others is key to our self-awareness, because our own hearts can deceive us. At times we can see others' situations accurately, but we don't see ourselves with the same keen vision. It's hard to lead effectively when our personal vision is clouded. The Scriptures put it this way:

> "The heart is hopelessly dark and deceitful,
>   a puzzle that no one can figure out.
> But I, GOD, search the heart
>   and examine the mind.
> I get to the heart of the human.
>   I get to the root of things.
> I treat them as they really are,
>   not as they pretend to be."
>
>   (Jeremiah 17:9–10, MSG)

We need God's word to discern our hearts—to show us what is inside of them. We also need others to help draw these things out of our hearts as they speak the truth to us in love.

She let others into her life.

When we are not aware of our "default" modes of operation, our character issues, and our sinful tendencies, we will continue to make the same mistakes and think with the same unspiritual thought patterns. We will get defensive when these things are pointed out to us. The people we interact with the most are usually aware of these tendencies— yet we ourselves can too easily miss what is obvious to others.

What keeps us from being self-aware? We block self-awareness when we do not invite others into our lives to help us see ourselves, or when we push people away. Perhaps our own feelings of shame, guilt, pain, and worthlessness hinder us from being open to seeing what we are really like. Our "default" ways of thinking often come from the way we were raised and the examples we saw around us. We often see through "distorted eyes" when we have experienced neglect, abuse, anger, guilt, shame, or rejection. The truth we can learn from God's word and from spiritual people helps us have the "good eyes" described in Matthew 6:22— thus giving us a clear perspective of ourselves. When we resist the truth about our lives, Satan blinds our minds (2 Corinthians 4:4). The Samaritan woman did not resist hearing the truth about her life. Although she needed to push through her questions about the "proper place of worship," she came to view her situation clearly. She faced the truth about herself and accepted it—and found that forgiveness, freedom, and acceptance were awaiting her.

What difference does it make to be a self-aware spiritual leader?

Knowing who we really are helps us to change. And once we see ourselves clearly, we can help others more completely, because we aren't so busy defending ourselves or remaining caught up in our own life traps. Are you a good listener, or do you do most of the talking? When you experience fear, do you tend to fight or flee? Are you quickly able to admit fault and apologize, or do you tend to shift blame and rationalize? Are you quicker to extend grace or to be judgmental? Do you tend to be a people-pleaser, or are you honest in what you say? Do you tend to ignore things you see in others, or are you quick to address them? Do you tend to enable others in their weaknesses, or do you call them to change? As you become more aware of your tendencies in these (and other) areas, you will become more effective in avoiding Satan's traps for your life, and will be better equipped to give others what they most need.

If the Samaritan woman had not put her jar down at the well and embraced the truth about herself, she would have walked away still thirsty, still longing for "living water." While she could have argued with Jesus, lied to him, ignored him or rationalized his words away, she chose to embrace the truth about herself. Because of this, not only was her life changed, but many others also came to know the Jesus she had met:

> Many of the Samaritans from that town believed in him because of the woman's testimony, "He told me everything I ever did." So when the Samaritans came to him, they urged him to stay with them, and he stayed two days. And because of his words many more became believers. (John 4:39–41)

- Can you describe your tendencies, including the answers to the questions listed in the previous section?
- Ask several people close to you how they view you in these areas. Does their view match yours?
- Can you describe someone who is not self-aware? How does interacting with them affect you?
- What is one way you can become more self-aware? How might this help you become a more effective spiritual leader?

Like the Samaritan woman, let us embrace the truth about ourselves and invite others into the deep places of our heart. Others will be amazed at the freedom we have found, and may in turn seek to know the One who set us free.

It is essential for a leader to be aware of both her strengths and her weaknesses. It is also possible for us to be too self-aware. I have to pray for God to keep me out of his way.

—Gloria Baird, Los Angeles, California

Self-awareness first humbles us—then teaches us how to discern what is best (Philippians 1:9–10)

—Virginia Lefler, Chicago, Illinois

Each time I think I have self-awareness, I find out something new about myself. I must continue to be a learner—to remember that I do not have all the answers, to keep being open with those directly involved in my life, and to be willing to take feedback. When I approach others from a "not-knowing" posture, I am more receptive to really hearing them and to putting myself in their shoes.

—Karen Louis, Singapore

We may have many pearls of wisdom to share with others, but if we deliver our advice in the wrong way or are harsh when we share it, then others won't want to listen to us. We have to be aware "in the moment" of how we are coming across. Is our listener "pulling a face" at us because we are accusing them, or are we boring them as we speak too much? Can we change how we handle a conversation mid-stream as we learn new conflicting information? This may completely alter a predetermined course of action. (Proverbs 18:17). It takes humility for us to change our minds.

—Caron Vassallo, Melbourne, Australia

We all need at least one or two sisters in our life who will tell us when we have spinach between our teeth or sin in our heart.

—Jeanie Shaw, Burlington, Massachusetts

PROFILE

Michelle Yaros, Missouri: Self-Awareness

by Michelle Yaros

There are times when our faith is deeply tested, and we grow more than we could have imagined. When we are aware of our own temptations and weaknesses, we allow God to strengthen and comfort us. Michelle Yaros has grown through her challenges, and because of this, her life has been able to affect many others. Michelle's challenges will inspire you to draw closer to God.

Throughout our spiritual walk, we have many conversion experiences. My first was when I became a disciple at the age of eighteen. When I was baptized, I was overjoyed to find my relationship with God and to see what God would have in store for me. It was obvious how God had orchestrated people to come into my life to show me the way to him. My faith was fresh, my heart was eager, and my life had found new purpose.

Then life came along…college, dating, career, marriage, and children. To some extent, being a disciple became more of a habit and a lifestyle for me. I often thought that because I had chosen to follow God, life should be good and the storms minimal. But that isn't always the case. After twenty years of marriage in God's kingdom, I found myself a divorced single mother of three teenagers. I was crushed. The landscape of my life and spirituality had taken a drastic change.

As I cried out to God, I realized that I had a decision to make. I could blame God, become bitter, and potentially destroy the faith of my children; or I could cling to the Word, open my heart to the women around me, and beg God to carry me. I chose the latter.

I definitely couldn't see how I was going to fare in this storm. Through my tears, I begged God to speak to me through his word. Each day as I read, God showed me that he could identify with every emotion I was experiencing. Rejection? Betrayal? Loneliness? Yes, Jesus had been there.

I saw how God hurt with me, and the Psalms became a balm for my broken heart. I would call the women in my life and share my attitudes, feelings, and tears. They patiently listened and cried with me. I borrowed their faith because mine was weak. They helped me to stay focused on God, and to trust that he was preparing my children and me for something better.

I begged God to not let the circumstances shipwreck my children's faith. My heart was breaking as I watched my kids wrestle with why this had happened. I begged God to work in their hearts as they navigated through a situation that most "Kingdom Kids" (kids who grow up in the church) will never experience. But I had to realize that God was also preparing their hearts through this storm.

As time moved on, I also had to look at my heart. Relationships don't occur in a vacuum. What was God trying to show me about relationships in general, and especially with him? I began to realize that I had hurt God by allowing the circumstances of life rob me of complete intimacy with him. This conversion brought me to a deeper understanding and tenderness with God than I had ever experienced during my long walk as a disciple.

Wounds take time to mend. Seeing how God has provided for us and carried us through this experience continually helps my heart to heal. I have watched my children grow in their relationship with God, and they have felt the love and support of his kingdom like never before. As with any conversion, the power is in seeing God transform the hearts of others. Despite our family's difficult circumstances, the power of Jesus' sacrifice moved the heart of my seventeen-year-old daughter, and I was able to baptize her into Christ. I could feel God embrace me, and I knew all the pain and tears had been worth it.

Despite the storm, I have learned to embrace the struggle. While it has been the most difficult thing I have ever experienced, I would not change it. The conversion in my heart and my daughter's heart are too valuable. I continue to pray for humility and to be an example of love and faith. I have learned that I cannot control what happens to me, but I have the Spirit to guide me as I deal with it. I have chosen God and his sacrifice—they are all I need.

CHAPTER NINE

Martha: Leadership and Hospitality
Teresa Fontenot

Luke 10:38-41; John 11-12

Have you ever been caught by the camera in a very unattractive pose, only to have it displayed in some form on social media? Or even worse, have you been caught on video in a moment when you are completely overwhelmed and "venting" on those you love the most? How would you like to have that moment in time preserved for all posterity? How humiliating to have this as part of your legacy. We catch a glimpse of Martha at just such a time. She probably had many days that ran smoothly, but the Bible gives us a snapshot from when she was having one of "those days," and it is indelibly printed on our minds. Although Martha may have cringed whenever she remembered this moment in her life—surely it was her "most embarrassing moment"—I am so grateful that God preserved it to teach us even today.

Hospitality of heart

Martha received the word "Jesus is coming," and she began to prepare. Martha was a woman of action. She was a wonderful hostess because she anticipated the needs of her guests and made them feel special. It gave her real delight to express her love to Jesus and his disciples by opening her home to them. She wanted everything to be perfect. She had seen to the preparation for the bread—grinding, mixing, kneading, and baking. It generally took three hours to produce enough flour to feed a household of five to six people.[9] An animal had been prepared to eat. The water had been drawn, the house cleaned, all the utensils and dishes washed. There was plenty of wine. She had prepared bedding for a large number to stay the night, in case all twelve disciples came along with Jesus. All bowls and towels were ready for foot-washing and hand-washing. She must have a comfortable place for Jesus to sit and teach—with refreshments, of course. Martha was a flurry of activity and excitement.

Martha was the first to greet Jesus after he had walked all day uphill from Jericho, and she welcomed him into her home with a kiss. The home of Martha,

Mary and Lazarus was one of the few places where Jesus could get away from constant demands. They were the closest thing he had to family. In their home, he knew he would always be accepted and could truly relax. This was the place where the only expectation was to meet *his* needs.

Martha and Mary both had passionate and generous hearts. Martha was passionate about hospitality. Taking care of her guests was of paramount importance to her. Mary, of course, made Jesus feel at home in a completely different way. Among the Jews there was a saying in circulation: "Let your house be a meeting place for the rabbis, and cover yourself in the dust of their feet, and drink in their words thirstily."[10] Together Martha and Mary fulfilled this proverb. They were both a great help to Jesus' ministry.

Traveling in Jesus' day was dangerous, and so hospitality could be a matter of life and death. The land was rugged and the temperature could be extreme. Inns were often dubious places where prostitution was part of the system. This may have been why Jesus told his disciples to stay in private homes (Matthew 10:11), and why it was so important that Christians "practice hospitality" toward one another (in Romans 12:13, the word *practice* means "to pursue"). The word *hospitality* in Greek is *philoxenia*, meaning "a love to strangers."[11] Hospitality was particularly needed by preachers of the time who had given up their livelihood so that they could preach the gospel. They were to be offered hospitality for several days, and then encouraged to move on to another place (e.g., Acts 9:43; 16:15; Romans 16:2). To be recognized as a leader in the church, you were (and are) expected to be hospitable (1 Timothy 3:2; Titus 1:8). Even an enemy could not be allowed to die of hunger. Paul wrote, "If your enemy is hungry, feed him" (Romans 12:20). If a person came within one's tent or home, he was absolutely safe under the protection of the family. In the East, even today, to invite someone to a meal was to extend an honor, an offering of peace, trust, and forgiveness. You also never knew whether you might be entertaining an angel (Hebrews 13:2).

Diabolical distractions

Mary was completely captivated by Jesus' teaching, but the Bible tells us that Martha "was distracted by all the preparations that had to be made." *Distracted* meant that Martha was being pulled away. She was too busy to give her full attention to Jesus' words. Martha obviously longed to be sitting at Jesus' feet with her sister, but she felt compelled to oversee the meal. After all, from the greeting to the final course, Martha wanted everything to be done well. Mary, however, picked up on the mood of Jesus, and knew that he would prefer fellowship to an elaborate spread of food. But Martha became upset with the situation. It is painful to imagine this scene:

Martha comes into the room, stands before Jesus, interrupts his teaching, in the midst of his disciples, to ask Jesus a question and give him a command. She asks, "Lord, don't you care that my sister has left me to do the work by myself?" In her distress, Martha questions Jesus' love for her. Perhaps he just can't see what is going on. She couldn't be more wrong, but unfortunately, she doesn't stop there. Her emotion has completely overtaken her reason, and so she commands Jesus to tell her sister to help her serve!

Martha gave into her anxiety and stepped out of bounds. The sad thing is, she probably felt completely justified—she expected Jesus to rebuke Mary. After all, Martha wanted to enjoy the company of their guests, too. She wanted to hear the stories and wisdom that always came with a visit from Jesus. And anyway, wasn't it inappropriate for Mary to put herself on equal footing with the male disciples by sitting at Jesus' feet?

The whole situation just angered and frustrated Martha. Martha needed to learn, as David wrote in Psalm 37:8, "do not fret—it leads only to evil"; or maybe the wisdom of Proverbs 17:1: "Better a dry crust with peace and quiet than a house full of feasting, with strife." The solution to Martha's problem was not for Mary to help serve. When you are serving the Lord, there is more on the menu than good food. When you are distracted, something must take precedence before we can regain focus. Distraction divides. Jesus helped Martha find clarity.

Although Jesus could have rebuked Martha for her disrespect, he was extremely gentle toward her. By saying her name twice, he was very personal in the way he sought her attention. He looked past her words and into her heart. He understood what she was feeling. Her intentions were good, but she had been pulled away from her desire to show love to strangers. The next time we see Martha is after Lazarus has died (John 11). Always the one to welcome, in spite of her grief, Martha goes out to greet Jesus when she hears he is coming. They have a deeply spiritual exchange, and Martha proclaims her faith that Jesus is the Son of God. It is a great moment.

Unfortunately, Martha, once again feels the need to enlighten Jesus. Ever practical, she is compelled to explain to him the process of a decaying body. After this length of time, there would be a bad odor, not to mention the fact that Jesus would become unclean as well. Martha does not want Jesus to suffer that kind of discomfort. (Her heart of hospitality was always to take care of others and make them comfortable, even though she sometimes went about it the wrong way.) Martha has no idea of the miracle that she is about to behold. Within minutes, she will be greeting her "dead" brother Lazarus, now living and breathing!

The soul of a servant

Jesus comes one last time to his "home away from home" in Bethany on his way to his death (John 12). A dinner is given in Jesus' honor, with Lazarus in attendance. The Bible says simply that "Martha served" (v. 2). It records no distraction, no distress, and no complaints. Perhaps Martha has finally learned to enjoy loving the Lord with all her soul. She loves to serve. It seems that she no longer compares or resents the way in which Mary offers her soul to Jesus. In Martha's practical mind, it must seem an extravagant expression to pour out thousands of dollars of perfume on Jesus' feet. But she doesn't say a word. Perhaps Martha has finally learned that hospitality is loving others. To honor Jesus, it is fitting to offer "extreme" hospitality.

Opening our homes and opening our hearts to strangers is what makes them become our friends. Martha was not afraid to open her home and her life for all to see, to the glory of God. We do not know what she served for dinner and we do not know what Jesus was teaching Mary and the disciples. But we do learn something about the genuineness of the love expressed in Martha's home. It was not a perfect expression of love, but it was authentic. Jesus only wanted the sisters to give their best, in heart and action. Martha learned this lesson well.

Our hospitality is meant to be the best we can offer. (Of course, we should always remain open to seeing the ways we can improve.) The menu should always include a large portion of the generous love of God. We can then serve a meal of "peace" and not "panic." We want our guests to leave feeling accepted and comforted, just as Jesus felt in Martha's home. Jesus wants us to enjoy eternal life now and later. When we are done offering hospitality here on earth, we will get to enjoy God's hospitality at a Great Banquet!

Consider your heart of hospitality:

- Why is it so important to excel in offering hospitality, especially if you are a leader?
- How often do you "pursue" the "love of strangers"? Is it your habit to be hospitable? Do you open your home to someone new every week? Every month?
- What would an outside observer see in you as you cope with life's schedules, commitments, and pressures? Would you remind them more of Martha or Mary? And how does this reflect on your relationship with Jesus?

- List some of the ways you want to learn and improve in your hospitality.

Let us all embrace hospitality, but do so remembering why we do it. Let us never become so consumed by what is on the table that we forget the people around it, and the God above it.

Hospitality isn't just about inviting someone into your home; it's about inviting them into your life.
—Linda Brumley, San Diego, California

Inviting people in to see our homes and our families is one of the greatest ways to share God with others. Sometimes a meal opens someone's heart—enabling you to have a great conversation that can make a real difference in their life. I hope people feel a sense of peace and warmth when they have been in my home.
—Chris Fuqua, Los Angeles, California

I love the way our physical family is like a microcosm of the church family! Our homes should be places of warmth and acceptance. Experiencing hospitality in a Christian home is often the training ground for future families that will glorify God.
—Geri Laing, Lake Worth, Florida

Keep your home tidy so you can be hospitable quickly.
—Roberta Balsam, Chicago, Illinois

Hospitality is a great kindness that speaks a lot about your heart.
—Virginia Lefler, Chicago, Illinois

Practicing hospitality is one way to show friendship, warm reception, sharing of food or whatever the need—no matter whether it is a cup of tea or coffee, a meal, or even a bed to sleep on. Hospitality is a practical way to show our love to God out of the overflow of our heart, and to show gratitude that is not self-motivated and conditional (Matthew 25:34–40). The practice of hospitality has continued to help me win new friendships inside and outside of the church, smooth some difficult relationships, and inspire disciples to learn and practice hospitality as an evangelistic tool.
—Elizabeth Sinn, Hong Kong, China

PROFILE

Ruby Ulm, Kansas City, USA and London, England: Hospitality

by Nadine Templer, New Delhi, India

"When life gives you lemons, make lemonade!" Those were some of Ruby Ulm's favorite words—and she lived by them. Ruby passed away several years ago. Her life is a testimony to what it means to be a giver, no matter our personal circumstances.

I met Ruby when I was a young Christian in London. I had only been a Christian for a short time when someone told me that Ruby, a single woman in the church, had paid for me and a couple of other sisters to fly to the States to attend the Boston Women's Day—a trip that changed my life. It gave me a vision to do great things for God as a young woman. I will be forever thankful to Ruby for giving me that opportunity.

Years later, my family moved to Kansas City for a few months, after facing persecution on the mission field. There we were reunited with Ruby, who had moved to the States to get married. What a joy it was to live again in the same city as Ruby! She opened her heart and home to me and my family, letting us use her car, and even babysitting for us. I remember the many meals she cooked for us, the countless ways she made everything special, and how she opened her home to people both inside and outside the church. At a time when my family was hurting after leaving India, it was so comforting to enjoy Ruby's hospitality.

I also remember how Ruby's house was such a *home*. It was tastefully decorated, clean, and welcoming. In spite of the care she took to make her home attractive, she did not mind the crowds that would often invade her private space. She always had a ready smile on her face. In London and in Kansas City, Ruby's home was often used for staff meetings, leaders' meetings, women's groups, and many other gatherings.

Decades later, now that I am a homemaker, I cherish my memories in Ruby's home. They call me higher and spur me on to give—and to open my own house to others. As we prepare meals for large groups, host numerous meetings in our front room, and give up our bedrooms to host guests, I am encouraged by the memories Ruby created for me.

Most of the people who knew and loved Ruby recall her hospitality, her generosity, and her wisdom. What many people did not know is how courageous she was. Ruby loved people, especially children—yet God never gave her children of her own. So many women face that pain, as month after month their hopes are shattered. It is very hard for someone who has such a big heart to not have a child with whom they can share their love. For many of us, undergoing such disappointment and heartache would have led to resentment towards God, or even bitterness. Not Ruby. She shared about her sadness, but she graciously accepted God's will for her life. I never heard her complain about not having children of her own. Instead, she "adopted" other people's children and treated the young people in the church as her children. When God blessed her with a second marriage later in life—to Richard Ulm, a wonderful man—God also blessed her with several stepchildren and grandchildren.

Ruby's understanding of God enabled her to smile and remain calm through experiences that could have made her negative. She refused to yield to faithlessness and bitterness, and always gave, no matter her circumstances. She is gone, but her legacy of hospitality and generosity lives on in the hearts of everyone who had the joy of knowing her.

CHAPTER TEN

Abigail: Leadership and Prudence
Jeanie Shaw

1 Samuel 25

Abigail was disturbed by the situation that had unfolded—and not just disturbed; she was afraid. She learned that King David had been rudely treated by her husband, Nabal. David had been kind to Nabal's shepherds and had asked for Nabal's hospitality in return. But instead of offering hospitality, Nabal gave out insults. Sadly, this did not surprise Abigail. She was accustomed to her husband's selfish behavior. He was wealthy but certainly not generous. He was successful in business, but mean and difficult in character. David was angry with Nabal's response, and he planned to attack and kill the men in Nabal's household. One of the servants advised Abigail of David's intent, and pleaded with Abigail to "think it over and do something." Her reputation was such that this servant believed she would know just what to say and what to do. Abigail, fearing that David would seek violent revenge upon her household, knew she had to act quickly—but she had to act wisely. Prudently.

Abigail had practiced prudence for a while. Being married to a man like Nabal—he was often arrogant, stubborn, and ungodly—had taught her wisdom and patience. This continual practice prepared her to respond without hesitation. She had learned to "walk the line" of standing up for what was true and right while still treating her husband with respect. She knew when to speak up and when to be silent. She knew (in the words of Kenny Rogers' famous country song) "when to hold 'em, when to fold 'em, when to walk away, and when to run."[12] This was not easy; it took prayer, consideration, and her own commitment to righteousness.

She realized she needed to address the situation at hand, but knew she must speak in a way that David could hear, even through his indignation. The tone of her voice, the words she used, and the way she presented herself would make a difference in the response she would get from the angry future king.

Studying people

Abigail had learned to study people. In this case, she realized that if David had asked for hospitality for his "crew," then they were probably hungry…and it's hard to reason with a group of hungry, grumpy men. She made delicious food—lots of it—and sent it on ahead of her as a peace offering. She then approached David and appealed to the good in him—appealing to his personal righteousness. Though David was a powerful man, she boldly reminded him to think about the future and his accountability before God. She pleaded with him not to repay evil for evil. She brought the best out of David, calling upon his desire to be faithful to God's truths.

Thinking it over

Our prudence can also make a difference in people's lives in ways we may never know. Prudence puts wisdom into practical application.

How do we show good judgment and dependence on God, as Abigail did, when the pressure is on us? Her wisdom, patience, and good judgment brought the best out of someone, and saved him from making a terrible mistake. Abigail took the time to consider how to calm David down and inspire him to do the right thing. From Abigail we see the importance of "thinking over" or considering the appropriate next steps we need to take in any situation. God tells us to first pray for wisdom and to trust that he will give it to us.

Abigail understood that poor timing can tempt even the good-hearted to do wrong! She sent her peace offering ahead first, to soften David up, then she herself approached him and slowly, graciously built her case, asking him to show mercy.

Abigail was also convinced that David, who was always striving to follow God, was still full of goodness even though he was angry (Romans 15:14)—she assumed the best, and then she helped to draw it out of him with a masterful speech.

Prudence recognizes that people are motivated differently at different times. In Hebrews 10:24, the Scriptures teach us to "consider how we may spur one other on toward love and good deeds." We learn how to approach people around us, and we also learn that some people are motivated differently from others. What motivates you may not be exactly the same for someone else. Some need a gentle word, while others won't get the message without the proverbial two-by-four hitting them between the eyes. Some are motivated and changed by a story or parable, and others by setting goals of accomplishment.

Reaching the heart

Abigail had learned how to approach different people. She had also learned how not to approach others—at first, she chose not to tell Nabal about her plan. She acted alone. And even after David and his men turned away and the crisis had ended, Abigail said nothing to her husband. She waited until the next morning, when he was sober, before telling him of the tragedy he'd nearly brought down upon their household.

As we grow in prudence, we learn to draw people out and help them make decisions that are righteous; we learn to appeal to their integrity. This takes listening to what others say, learning what is important to them, and asking questions that draw them out. Simple "yes or no" questions are not as likely to reach to the heart. The Scriptures teach us that the purposes inside of people are like "deep waters," and it takes a person of understanding to draw them out (Proverbs 20:5).

While as leaders we must continue to grow in prudence, it is also important to remember that a person's response to God's ways does not depend on us or on our wisdom. Each person is responsible for his or her own choices. We are merely vessels that God can use. God himself grants repentance, lest we rely on our own wisdom, and get prideful; or feel like we don't have enough wisdom, and get discouraged.

Prudence seeks to reach hearts with scriptures instead of just giving information. Prudence knows that when people turn to God they will be given what they need. They don't have to have all the answers.

How we say it is important

Abigail was careful in what she said *and* how she said it. In the same way, Jesus tells us, "The Father who sent me commanded me what to say and how to say it" (John 12:49). If Jesus was careful with his words, how much more must we be careful with what we say and how we say it!

Abigail approached David with food and gifts, and spoke to him personally. She did not send an emissary. It is all too easy in this era of digital communication to neglect taking the time to engage in personal conversation. When emotions run high, it is prudent to stay away from e-mails and texts—instead, pick up the phone or meet face to face.

Abigail did not approach David with blame or accusation. She was humble before him. Prudence is accompanied by humility. It is essential to listen first and draw conclusions later. We may be missing some important information, or "the other side of the story." As it says in Proverbs 18:17, "The first to present his case seems right, till another comes forward and questions him." Remember that people are doing what makes sense to them, so it's important to understand where they're coming from and why they are acting the way they are. When we respond based on principles of truth from God's word rather than our own opinions, we learn prudence.

Abigail did not know how David or Nabal would respond to her. She had the courage to step out in faith in the face of great risk, without support from her husband. It takes courage, prudence, and persistence to go alone and to keep doing good without encouragement from those close to us. But it can be done.

Abigail's prudence kept David from sinning, and kept her entire household from being killed. Never underestimate the power of this quiet quality—it might just save your life!

- What are some ways you can practice prudence?
- What are some situations where you need to approach different people in different ways?
- How do tone and word choice affect the way people hear you?
- When are you most fearful to approach someone and call them to righteousness? How might you best overcome that fear?

God did not forget Abigail, and he will not forget you. She was rewarded for her good judgment, righteousness, and courage. In the same way, if we cultivate the positive character traits that help us overcome problems, positive things will happen. They won't always be the positive things we want or expect, but God will always work to bring good out of any situation (Romans 8:28). If your husband is not a disciple, it may mean that if you persist in your example, he will become a new person in Christ. Or it may mean that you will grow in your character and wisdom, and become more like Christ because of persevering through a challenging situation. Our circumstances, like Nabal, may not change, but there is more to our story than mere circumstances. No matter what happens in life, if we continue to do good and grow in God's grace, by the power of God one day we will hear those long-awaited words from Matthew 25:21, "Well done, good and faithful servant!"

It takes patience to work with people who don't see things that are clear to us. Just saying our thoughts louder, or repeating ourselves, is not going to get through—and those strategies may actually backfire and cause us to be a stumbling block. We need to extend grace and pray for clarity and insight as we let the Holy Spirit do its work. As God worked in Paul's life, the scales fell off of his eyes and he saw himself and God. We need to pray for God to open people's eyes to the truth.

—Kim Evans, Philadelphia, Pennsylvania

I love studying the Proverbs, where there are many scriptures regarding our words. The older I get, the more I become grateful for what I have decided not to say. Holding my tongue is a lot harder than saying everything that comes to mind.

—Chris Fuqua, Los Angeles, California

As you share with others, teach them to think for themselves and to learn to apply the Scriptures to their lives in practical ways. It's easier to skip this step and just speak, instead of ensuring that others know the truth behind what you are saying. Ask questions such as, "What do you think? What would you do? Why would you respond that way? What scriptures can you think of that apply to this situation?"

— Jeanie Shaw, Burlington, Massachusetts

My mom always had a framed quote that meant a lot to me. It said, "It's what you learn, after you know it all, that counts." I think as a leader, it is so vital to have the heart to keep learning new things to make you better in the ministry, in life, and in family.

—Laura Fix, Londonderry, New Hampshire

PROFILE

Catherine, Singapore: Prudence

by Joyce Ng and Chew Wai Yee, Singapore

"Catherine" (name changed to protect her family's privacy) was baptized as a teenager, and from the very beginning, she had tremendous zeal for God. When she was sixteen and someone asked her to lead her first group Bible discussion, she got so excited that she accidentally walked into a glass door! She matured emotionally and spiritually, and grew into a godly young Christian woman—beautiful on the outside and inside. This wonderful sister was full of expectation for what her Christian life would bring in the future, and assumed things would follow a certain script. As she grew in her faith, enjoying her Christian life, Catherine had dreams of doing great things for God.

After a few years, she was married in the church to a disciple. As a young newlywed, she envisioned a beautiful life; she had always wanted to serve God and the church alongside her husband. Unfortunately, a few years into their marriage, Catherine's husband left the Lord. He also lost his zest for life. He could not hold a job, and he became reclusive. This was not what Catherine had dreamed of or expected. Catherine now had to support their family financially, emotionally, and spiritually. In spite of all these challenges, Catherine is an example of godliness among the young mothers of the Singapore church. She is incredibly joyful, serving, and giving. She never holds back her time, energy, or money from the Lord. Catherine has decided in her heart that while she continues to pray for her husband to come back to the Lord, she will not stop allowing God to use her in every way.

Catherine is often seen serving other people in the church with her two young children in tow. She now leads a ministry of sisters with diverse needs, and they all look up to her faith and convictions. She studies the Bible with other women, and she helps to strengthen struggling sisters—all while being a great mom and a great wife. Even as she leads other sisters, she constantly seeks advice on her schedule and how to better meet the needs of her own husband

and children. At various times, she engages other brothers to reach out to her husband. As a mom, she understands the need for her children to have strong adult role models and peer relationships, and she makes arrangements to ensure this happens.

At work, Catherine is a shining light, earning the trust of her boss and colleagues. Through her example of joy and resilience, Catherine recently helped her colleague, who is a single mom, to turn to Christ.

The most outstanding thing about Catherine is her quiet and gentle spirit, and the way she remains ever so respectful of her husband. She has resolved not to nag or be bitter—despite her challenges. Many women are convicted by the way she never complains about her life, even though they see her struggle financially and physically.

Catherine would admit that there have been many moments when she has had to wrestle emotionally and spiritually while juggling all the needs and responsibilities in her life. That's when her pure-hearted devotion to God sets in, driving her to go to God in prayer and meditation of his word. She spends time journaling her thoughts and surrendering them to God.

Her humility is not only seen in her reliance on God, but also in her willingness to allow other sisters to give her feedback. She constantly shares about her struggles, and perseveres with her challenges. This endearing quality has helped her to grow "from strength to strength" (Psalm 84:7) and inspires other women who go through similar challenges in life. Catherine embraces the Bible's call to women in 1 Peter 3:6—she does what is right and does not give way to fear.

CHAPTER ELEVEN

The Proverbs 31 Woman: Leadership and Organization
Robin Williams
Proverbs 31:10-31

She moved quickly as her child called out to her. Her daughter was not feeling well this morning, and she made sure she had plenty of water and herbs to settle her stomach. Her other children were already doing their morning chores. She had begun the day reading scriptures from the Torah and singing songs. She smiled as she heard her children singing these same songs as they worked. Today was a full day, as usual. She would still need to sell some of her wares. She had one offer on a field that was still under negotiation. She gave the young servant girl who she was training a list of vegetables to prepare, and showed her how to knead the bread. She took her cloth into her sick daughter's room and told stories of great men and women of God to her daughter as she sewed.

Who was this woman? When I read about her, I am always mesmerized by her indomitable spirit. I ask myself, how did she do it? What enabled her to accomplish so much in her life? She's the mother of all mothers, the wife of all wives, the queen of organization—the woman we all dream of becoming—but often feel like we will never be. But in order to make progress we must start with a dream—an ideal. The Proverbs 31 woman stands as that ideal.

She has no name, but some scholars think she may have been based on Bathsheba, because King Lemuel may have been another name for King Solomon, Bathsheba's son. We can't be sure; but if so, then she epitomizes the transforming power of true repentance. If so, she transformed from a woman caught up in a scandal to a woman who exemplifies godly womanhood.

How did this woman's organizational skills enable her to create such a wonderful life for her husband, her family, her household, and herself?

Her convictions were based on the fear of God.

> Charm is deceptive, and beauty is fleeting;
> but a woman who fears the LORD is to be praised.
> (Proverbs 31:30)

When we fear the Lord, we gain insight into our lives and how we should live them. This affects our words and our actions. It shows how much we need God, and that without him we can do nothing.

The amazing thing about the fear of God is that it takes away all our other fears. As David says in Psalm 34, "I sought the LORD, and he answered me; he delivered me from all my fears" (v. 4). And when we fear the Lord, we lack nothing (vv. 9, 10).

Fearing God is love for God in its purest form. It is the beginning of everything good. As David continues his song in Psalm 34:11–14, he says that to fear the Lord we must keep our tongue from evil, avoid lies, turn from evil, do good, and seek and pursue peace. If Bathsheba is the woman depicted in Proverbs 31, she would certainly have a deep appreciation for God's mercy. Perhaps God spared her so she could become an example for all of us.

Like Bathsheba, we also need his amazing grace to save us from all of our sins—the grace we received when we were buried with Christ in baptism and raised to a new and transformed life. This grace, coupled with a healthy fear cradled deep in our hearts and minds, is what enables us to do the good God created us to do.

How does fearing God relate to being organized? Primarily, for me, it means that I want to be my best for God. I respect him, and so I want to offer him my best—and it takes organization to be my best. The organization of my life is a by-product of my gratitude for God and his grace for me. It reveals my priorities, my heart, and my dependence on him.

When I realize how much God has done for me, I am grateful, and I want to do as much as possible for him. Since there is so much I want to do for God, I need him to help me be organized. It's as simple as that. There are a lot of good things I *could* do, so, it takes prayer and dependence on God to determine what he wants me to do. My fear of God—my respect for his wisdom—makes me want to do the things he wants me to do, not just what I want to do. What are some of the things he wants us to do, as shown by the life of the Proverbs 31 woman?

- Take care of our husbands (vv. 11–12, 23)
- Take care of our families (vv. 15, 21)

- Take care of ourselves (vv. 17, 22, 25–26)
- Be productive by working hard (vv. 13–19, 24)
- Do good deeds for others (vv. 20, 24)
- Teach others (v. 26)
- Have no fear (vv. 21, 25)

Organization requires delegation.

The Proverbs 31 woman was an outstanding delegator. As she parceled out duties, everyone felt needed, and she was able to pass on her skills. It often feels easier to try to do everything by ourselves. But when we do this, we actually limit how much can get done. Other people don't feel needed, and they don't get the chance to learn.

As young children, we organize life in a very simple way: What am I going to do today? As we grow older, life has to be organized, planned, and thought out in order to be productive and fulfilling—not quite as spontaneous and spur of the moment as it once was. We have more people depending on us, we have more responsibilities, and we need to make money to take care of our family's needs. It's not that we can't be spontaneous; it just takes organization to be able to have the time to be spontaneous.

Delegation means I depend on others to help me do what is needed. This woman had servant girls who helped her do things around her house so she could focus on tasks that others could not do. Most modern moms don't have servant girls—a few of us may have a maid service or a nanny—but even if you have no professional help, remember, you do have children! Of course, they are not our slaves, but we should train them to be helpful around the house. They should be where we first practice delegation. Like the Proverbs 31 woman's household, it's a two-way street: we provide for them, and they help around the house. Entrusting our children with chores and responsibilities is not only good for their character; it also enables us to do more for the people around us and thus accomplish more. We may also delegate certain tasks to people like babysitters, tutors, teachers, and employees.

This woman not only delegates and depends on others to help her, but she sets the right example for her family and the people around her as she works vigorously with her own strong arms. She watches over her household, knows what is going on, and is pleased with the results. She is prepared for the unexpected. She depends on others to supply her with the things she needs—food, wool and flax, scarlet and purple cloth, and fine linen. She depends on merchants from whom she buys, sells, and trades as she runs her business. Depending on others is a graceful art. Knowing how to "give orders" with grace can only be learned from God. He's the one who does it best. When we fear him, he will give us the grace and wisdom to do so.

It takes time and thought to get organized. The Proverbs 31 woman planned her time. She planned to rise early and stay up late. She considered a field and bought it out of the earnings of her own hands. She made and sold things so that she could buy that extra field she needed to provide for her family. All these things take time and planning. To do them well, she had to plan ahead and make the most of her time.

Organization leads to happiness.

When I am organized and know what to expect, I am happy. Surprises, for the most part, should be for parties—not daily life. If your life is organized, you can enjoy occasional interruptions. Organization helps us be prepared for the unexpected. Strength and dignity are by-products of our organization. It enables us to laugh at the days to come because we're prepared for whatever comes our way. We can enjoy the day no matter how hard the rain or deep the snow. When we're organized, we are free to serve others—and serving others makes us happier people.

If we are unhappy, overwhelmed, and burdened, then perhaps we are focusing on the wrong things. We need to fear God by realizing how much we need him, and focusing on the things that are important to him. This may mean getting rid of superfluous additions to our lives. When we fear God and prioritize and organize our life the way he wants us to, the rest of our life turns out better (Matthew 6:33).

Some of us may find organization overwhelming and intimidating. We can feel like others do this easily, but for us it does not come naturally. Strive to make progress in one or two areas at a time. Maybe you can begin by making a schedule for your daily routines, or cleaning one room at a time. Find others who are strong in organization and ask them to give you helpful tips. With practice, organization is a skill that will improve over time as your responsibilities in life and leadership increase.

We may not get some things in our schedule done, but that's okay because God is in control—not us. The Proverbs 31 life is not about perfection, but about priorities. When we learn how to organize our lives according to God's priorities, then our life will not only honor him, but will bring us fulfillment and bring joy to all who know us.

- Are you still depending on God like you did at first—praying and studying his word like you couldn't breathe if you didn't?
- What would God have you prioritize as the most important things in your day or week? Does your daily schedule reflect those priorities? How much attention are you giving to your prayer life and Bible study, time with the family of God, and your mission to share God's word with others?
- What are ways you currently use your time that don't reflect the priorities God calls you keep? Can you simplify your life or schedule in any way, cutting out superfluous things that distract you from what's most important?
- Do you teach your family to love God first by the priorities you keep and the example you set?
- How can you delegate tasks more effectively?

The Proverbs 31 woman accomplished all the things she did because she feared God, loved God, and put him first in her everyday life. When God comes first, our schedule and organization will reflect godly priorities, and we will be like this woman—our children will call us blessed and our husband will praise us at the city gates.

> "Many women do noble things,
>   but you surpass them all."
> Charm is deceptive, and beauty is fleeting;
>   but a woman who *fears the LORD* is to be praised.
> Give her the reward she has earned,
>   and let her works bring her praise at the city gate."
>   (Proverbs 31:29–31, emphasis added)

To keep all the parts working effectively together, there must be order. The order also brings peace.

—Teresa Fontenot, Sydney, Australia

Live balanced days. If every day includes the following five things, your influence will be lasting. First, spend time with God. Second, spend time with your family (or roommates). Third, spend time with disciples. Fourth, spend time with the lost, and fifth, spend time on your physical world. (God put us in a physical world that needs tending.) When one area is discouraging, another area will encourage you. Some days require more times spent in one area over another—but even a simple prayer or call in an area that is lacking will keep momentum going.

—Kim Evans, Philadelphia, Pennsylvania

Return emails and calls promptly.

—Roberta Balsam, Chicago, Illinois

Take a time each week to talk and plan ahead as a married couple. In your prayer ministry, use the help of a schedule so different people and ministries can be prayed for on different days.

— Irene Koha, Lexington, Massachusetts

I like to look at organizing events as a way of extending hospitality, a way to "love strangers" and introduce them to Jesus. From the moment that a stranger enters the room, how can we facilitate warm welcomes, great conversations and shared stories that speak about changed lives and new beginnings? We don't organize for organization's sake—we do it so that events can accomplish their true purpose: touching hearts for God. And remember…the most important "thing" at any event is the people.

—Pat Brush, Miami, Florida

Contrary to a popular song, Sunday mornings are not always easy. Prepare well beforehand to make it as stress-free as possible. Then you can actually prepare your mind and heart to worship God with your brothers and sisters. When our children were young, we sang with them on the way to church and prayed together about the day.

—Jeanie Shaw, Burlinton, Massachusetts

PROFILE

Rachel Louis, Singapore: Organization
by Rachel Louis

Rachel Louis is a young woman in Singapore who gets a lot done for God and for people. An aspiring teacher, she grew up in different cities around Southeast Asia, and in her teenage years, she began participating in and organizing various programs to educate underprivileged children. Rachel is presently an undergraduate studying English linguistics in one of the world's top universities on a full scholarship, and on top of her studies, she finds the time to mentor other young women to help them grow spiritually. She is grateful to her parents for passing down their love for helping others and their skills with time management. This wise-beyond-her-years young lady offers words of wisdom for all "busy people," showing us ways we can serve, no matter what our stage in life. (Rachel originally wrote this article for the Web site www.wikigives.com.)

We all have a desire to do good. We applaud those who dedicate their lives to helping the less fortunate, and we hold philanthropists in high regard. In an ideal world, we would even want to be one of them. Yet for many of us, it remains a mere ideal because we simply have no time.

In a world run by practicality and efficiency, volunteering is not exactly on the top of our list of priorities. It can appear overly time-consuming, requiring too much hard work. While much of traditional volunteerism does admittedly involve a certain amount of commitment, there are other ways to serve the communities around us without having to set aside a lot more additional time. Here are five ways to integrate volunteerism into your busy life.

Integrate volunteering with your hobby.

Most of us have a couple of hobbies and interests that we engage in from time to time. Instead of spending a couple of hours on them, why not "kill two birds with one stone" and volunteer while pursuing your interest? Musicians on Call (www.musiciansoncall.org) is an organization in the US that sends volunteer musicians to play live music at the bedside of hospital patients, to lift their spirits. WriteGirl (www.writegirl.org) is an organization that offers writing workshops and one-on-one mentorships to empower teenage girls who would not otherwise have such opportunities.

There's something special about being able to share what you love with people to whom you are trying to *show love*. These are only two of many organizations out there that could offer you a chance to do good and have fun doing what you love at the same time.

Take a volunteer vacation.

What are you doing for your next family holiday? Speaking from personal experience, there are few things that can bond a group of people better than volunteering together in a foreign country. Having a common goal, going through the same experiences, and ultimately growing as individuals together will create family ties that last.

Try microvolunteering.

This is a recently coined term to describe a form of volunteerism that can be done from home, and very often in your pajamas. Different organizations such as Help from Home (www.helpfromhome.org) and Skills for Change (www.skillsforchange.com) provide an online platform for nonprofit organizations to request help from online volunteers. From Webcam-mentoring an AIDS-affected teenager in Africa to designing a fundraising poster for an elderly care center, there is a wide range of both one-off and long-term opportunities for volunteers who might not be able to commit a lot of time, or volunteer in person. Users can sift through available opportunities according to their own interests, skill sets, and commitment levels to find the right fit.

Take little steps.

There is a common misconception that if you volunteer, it should be for a great, noble cause such as ending world hunger, or solving the problem of poverty. While such lofty ambitions are indeed valuable, there is also much to be done in one's own backyard. For instance, my father recently discovered that we have an elderly neighbor living in a unit above us who makes his living by collecting and selling discarded flyers. My father has made it a point to help the man gather recyclables to sell, in order to boost his modest income.

There are people all around us who might just slip under our radar, who could benefit from our help. It does not take much time to become aware of our immediate surroundings. Simply taking a few moments to talk to our neighbors might reveal someone in need, a gap to be bridged.

Find your calling.

I have known since I was twelve that my calling was in the classroom. I love to learn, and desire wholeheartedly for everyone to have a chance to learn to love it as well. So whenever the opportunity arises, I look out for education-related programs to serve. Over the years, I have worked with a number of organizations, and the ones that have resonated with me on a personal level were also the same ones with whom I had the best experiences volunteering. Honestly, when you find the right fit, volunteering could very well become so much a part of your life that time is no longer an issue.

Leadership

and

Conviction

CHAPTER TWELVE

Esther: Leadership and Vision
Tammy Fleming
The Book of Esther

A young woman sits in her cramped bedroom in her cousin's house—the only home she's ever known. In her delicate, trembling hand she holds a letter from the palace. Through a blur of tears, three words stand out: *Summons. Palace. Marriage.*

And a short time later, she takes one last, lingering look at her humble room before traveling to the palace to join a gaggle of gorgeous women, all vying for the attention of the king. At the gate, she waves good-bye to her cousin Mordecai, wondering when (and if) she will ever see him again.

There have been times, in reading the book of Esther, that I've found it difficult to make a personal connection with this beautiful young virgin who rose from obscurity to royalty and saved her people. Even today, her Arabian Nights fairy-tale story feels about as far away from my cold Monday morning in rainy, gritty Birmingham, England, as you can get.

But then I remember: Esther lost her parents when she was young. The Jewish rabbinical literary tradition speculates that perhaps Esther's father died during her mother's pregnancy, and that Esther's mother died during childbirth.[13] Only God knows what really happened—but it provides one bridge to Esther, anyway, for me. My mother passed away from colon cancer when I was twenty-four. I was an only child, my father having died twelve years earlier. Even though I was "orphaned" as an adult, when my mother died I felt suddenly vulnerable, adrift from my moorings. I had a new, unmistakable, surreal sense of being alone. And then there was that awful, deep, spiritual question to wrestle with: why did you let this happen to *me*, God?

I wonder how deeply this question was imbedded in Esther's psyche. Esther was born into a discouraging time for the people of Israel, when God was shifting the tectonic plates of history, approaching the end of the Old Covenant and the advent of the New—preparing the way for the new and better ministry of Jesus (Hebrews 8:6). The Jews' long-standing, uniquely favored relationship with God seems lost: They are exiled in a foreign land, separated from the values and customs of Yahweh. To say that this time of prolonged political, spiritual, and emotional upheaval was traumatic for Esther's people must be an understatement.

Imagine, too, what it must have been like for a young woman (probably between fifteen and twenty-five years old), raised with Old Testament Jewish values and doted upon by a protective father figure like Mordecai,[14] to be suddenly and forcibly removed from her home, perhaps surrounded by other exiled Jewish families—and taken into the harem of the king of Babylon. Whatever personal plans and dreams she might have had were derailed forever. The Septuagint says that Mordecai had intended one day to marry Esther himself;[15] but thanks to the king's command, she was now to be groomed as one of literally hundreds of women whose main occupation in life was to compete to provide erotic entertainment for an arrogant, lavish, selfish monarch, who had already had sex with hundreds of women, and would continue on with hundreds more. There was no guarantee, after her one night of intimacy with the king (which, by the way, made her a legal wife—no less than Hagar was a legal wife to Abraham), that she would ever be invited back, or that she would ever have the chance to marry anyone else.[16] She could even be given away on a whim as a gift to some other ruler, from some other distant land.

The royal harem was a glorified prison for Esther: closely and jealously guarded, no chance to come and go as she pleased. No one could see anyone in a harem unless first carefully examined by senior officials. The atmosphere around Esther was worldly, competitive, and dangerous. An ancient Persian harem was reputed to be "a notorious source of seditious plots."[17] When the palace doors closed behind Esther, they also closed on any hopes she'd once had of romance, personal dreams, or traditional Jewish family life.

Esther was helpless to stop the forces that were taking her life in a direction that she surely would not have chosen for herself. Don't we all know this feeling? What happens to our faith and our vision, our trust in God, in times when circumstances beyond our control turn against us? It can be easy to pull away from God, emotionally and practically. Even if I know in my head that I shouldn't think that he's aiming Bad Luck right at me as a punishment, in my heart I can withdraw, like a turtle pulling into his shell for self-protection.[18] Or I can become numb and paralyzed. Just waiting. Waiting for circumstances to become more favorable. Waiting for someone to tell me what to do.

I wonder if Esther was emotionally shut down at the time when God, through Mordecai, sent his life-changing message into her apartments in the harem, and called her into action.

We don't know what Esther's personality was like. Maybe she had a good self-image. Maybe she didn't—maybe she was an example of a beautiful woman who can't fathom that she is beautiful. She could've been shy and melancholy, or feisty and outgoing. She might have been depressed and afraid—even suicidal—when she was herded into the harem with dozens of other young women. Or maybe being chosen for the harem swept her up into the kind of glamor and adrenaline-rush that come from winning a modern reality TV show like *The X Factor*.

One thing seems sure: Mordecai's step-parenting had instilled in Esther something that made her stand out from the crowd, a strength of character that did not erode in the face of tough challenges or with the passage of time. Consider these two verses:

> When the turn came for Esther…to go to the king, she asked for nothing other than what Hegai, the king's eunuch who was in charge of the harem, suggested. And Esther won the favor of everyone who saw her (2:15).

> Esther had kept secret her family background and nationality just as Mordecai had told her to do, for she continued to follow Mordecai's instructions as she had done when he was bringing her up (2:20).

Esther spent many months in the harem (anywhere from one to three years) before her turn came to go to the king, and yet the pressure upon her did not lead her to abandon the convictions with which she had been raised. She was humble, submissive, obedient—and not only to Mordecai, who was deserving of her love and trust—but also to the foreign, morally questionable authorities suddenly in control of her life. Why would Esther be so trusting in such a monstrous situation? In spite of all that had happened to her and to her people, Esther must have clung to the belief that God was good and would protect and deliver her. Perhaps she did not envision a triumphant outcome for her life or her people, but she did keep her sights set on living righteously, and on God's faithfulness.

At the point when Haman convinces Xerxes to issue the decree to annihilate the Jews throughout their empire, Esther has been living in the harem for five to eight years (2:16; 3:7). A lot has changed in her life since she lived at home under Mordecai's spiritual guidance and protection. She's been away from a strong spiritual atmosphere for a long time. She's become sexually active.

She's had to transfer her submission and obedience to people who don't know God and don't have God's standard of morality. And then a life and death crisis hits. It takes a little convincing before she agrees to comply with Mordecai's plan to ask the king for help to repeal his murderous decree, but when she agrees, we gain some great insight into Esther's character and why God's favor followed her.

Esther 4:15¬–16 reads, "Then Esther sent this reply to Mordecai: 'Go, gather together all the Jews who are in Susa, and fast for me. Do not eat or drink for three days, night or day. I and my maids will fast as you do. When this is done, I will go to the king, even though it is against the law. And if I perish, I perish.' "

After several years in the harem, where presumably she is the only believer in Yahweh, it's clear that Esther still identifies herself with God's people when she says, "go and gather together all the Jews who are in Susa." She turns to God in fasting and prayer, and she must have shared her faith over the years with her Persian maids, to such an extent that she can spontaneously vouch for their willingness to pray and fast to Jehovah, right along with her.

This tells me that Esther continued to be faithful to God even while living in a world of compromise that was far from her ideal. Esther set herself up to be in a position to do a great thing for God by being faithful in little things. She continued in the convictions that Mordecai had instilled in her as a little girl, and did not stray from them in spite of tremendous pressure.

What about us? Am I as faithful now as I was as a young(er) woman and a new Christian, in the basic spiritual disciplines that I learned to put into place as I began to walk with Jesus every day?

What about prayer and fasting? Is this my first port of call when I know there is a big challenge looming in front of me? It is a detail not to be overlooked, that the game-changer in this story is a weapon that every one of us has at our disposal, no matter what our IQ, income, social status, physical abilities or disabilities: we can all pray, and we can all fast (if not from food, at least from something), and devote more time to prayer.

Prayer changes everything. I will never forget one particular prayer in August 1989 at the Boston World Missions Seminar—a prayer for the Berlin wall to fall. The wall fell just two months later, on November 9, 1989, paving the way for us to go with a mission team into Moscow and the Soviet Union in July, 1991. A month after my husband and I arrived in Moscow with the mission team, President Gorbachev was taken hostage, and tanks filled the streets. Not understanding the full extent of what was taking place, but sensing it was big, we called the newly-baptized Russian disciples and the mission team—a team comprised mostly of American teenagers—to prayer: every morning at six, we met in the woods on the outskirts of the city, where no one would find us, and we prayed. But that's not all—around the world, disciples of Jesus were praying for us! CNN helped keep our predicament on people's minds, showing round-the-clock news coverage of the demonstrations and protests and unrest all around us. Missionaries from most other denominations fled. The Embassy told us all to leave. We stayed. Within a few days, power passed to Boris Yeltsin, the USSR broke apart, and our little mission team continued to baptize—850 people in the first year. God did something amazing, and all we did was what anybody could do: we prayed, and invited people to come see what we do at church.

We saw the power of prayer, and the power of God's people united in prayer. Even though Esther was the only Jew in the palace, and had been alone in her faith for many years, she had a mature understanding about the way God created us to function interdependently, in community. In her time of need, she immediately mobilized the community of the people of God and also the community of the closest women around her in the harem, and got them all to fast and pray with her. She dared to ask. This too, is something all of us can do: just ask.

At the end of the day, nothing that Esther did was out of reach for any of us. During the course of her life, as she continued in the godly principles she had learned as a child, God was working powerfully in ways that were impossible for her to perceive. There was no way she could have known, the night that the king could not sleep, that God was working on her behalf (6:1). There was no way she could have known that just as the king realized that he owed Mordecai a huge debt of gratitude, Haman would enter the outer court of the palace to request Mordecai's execution (6:4). She didn't see it coming . . . but she saw what God did in the end. All this is written for our benefit—to show us that our powerful God is working miracles, if only we will continue to be faithful to what we already know.

- Have you ever felt that the conditions around you are so bad that God just can't possibly work any good?
- Do you try to handle hard things yourself? What can you learn from Esther's instinct to immediately call upon the Jews in Susa and her maids in the harem to pray and fast with her?
- Has it been a while since you fasted? Is there anything worrying you that you should be committing to God through prayer and fasting?

- Are you able to view your life—even the difficulties and heartaches—with eyes of faith?

Esther couldn't see the big picture of her life, and yet God had a plan that was so much bigger than she ever could have envisioned. Even when we can't see an overarching plan in what looks like defeat, or the hand of God in what feels like disaster, God is still at work. Let Esther inspire us to keep our eyes on God, and to view life (even with all its unexpected turns) by faith, not sight.

We want the one in front to see farther than anyone else. That is why they are in the front.

—Teresa Fontenot, Sydney, Australia

There is probably no greater privilege than being able to express vision to others. After all, it is amazing to me that God had a vision for my life—I'm just passing that on to someone else. People light up when you express that you have confidence that God wants more for them.

—Chris Fuqua, Los Angeles, California

Many women focus too easily on the negative areas of their lives. Instead of "camping out" on areas that need to change, give them a vision for what they can become. Help them envision their weaknesses becoming their strengths (2 Corinthians 12:9), and overcoming evil with good (Romans 12:21).

— Jeanie Shaw, Burlington, Massachusetts

There is a Chinese proverb that states, "It is possible to move a mountain by carrying away small stones." It made me think of Jesus' words in Matthew 17:20, "I tell you the truth, if you have faith as small as a mustard seed, you can say to this mountain, 'Move from here to there' and it will move. Nothing will be impossible for you." As we strive to encourage and give others vision for what God can do in their lives, often we must help them "move stones." As they become mature, they can remember the stones that have been moved and keep the vision of the "moved mountain" in front of them.

—Beth Buchholz, Pembroke, Massachusetts

Something that helps give my life vision is to focus on eternal things. The only real eternal thing here on earth is people—so people need to take priority over our temporal matters.

—Lisa Schnell, Methuen, Massachusetts

PROFILE

Mikki, China: Vision
by Jane Chin, Hong Kong

Miki became a disciple in the Taipei Church of Christ as a single woman in March of 1996. Having been humbled by life's challenging circumstances in the area of dating and family, Miki felt a depth of gratitude in being saved from darkness and an empty way of life. She embraced her newfound grace, and leapt at the chance and privilege to live for God's purposes and vision. As a very young Christian, Miki joined a new mission team to northeast China by the end of that same year. She left the comfort of home and family in Taipei and courageously moved with the mission planting to serve as a self-supporting intern. After being abundantly fruitful there, she answered yet another call in 1998 to move to another metropolis in eastern China. Again with a determined vision for God's purposes, Miki set her heart on pilgrimage (Psalm 84:5) and continued to work, serve, and bear fruit there. Since then, Miki has moved back to Taipei and then back to China twice; she has served in many capacities in the church—as a self-supporting intern, a paid intern, and now as a lay leader in an underground church, serving alongside her husband.

In the midst of life's unexpected circumstances, relationships, roles, and leadership transitions that can make our journey suddenly more complicated or disheartening, we may start to stumble in our vision as we become anxious, fearful, and perhaps lose our faith. Miki has been a great example of "going from strength to strength" (Psalm 84:7) because of her very simple convictions that it is not about us, but about the privilege of serving God's purposes in any capacity, and that the heart of leadership is leaving God's imprint on another's life.

Miki married in 1998, and she and her husband, Jimmy, now have two sons. Their oldest son has some learning challenges, and has needed special attention and treatment over the years. Because Miki and Jimmy have a tenacious heart for China missions, they have continually sought ways to support themselves so as not to become a financial burden to the China mission's finances. They have tried to invest and start many small business ventures in China that have incurred personal financial loss. Yet what is most commendable about their example is their faithful heart in trusting God without complaint or bitterness, and their consistent spirit of generosity toward the people around them, even during tough times. They have only now, in the past couple of years, built a small company that has just begun to break even.

In this backdrop of life on the mission field, they started to lead an underground church in eastern China as "tentmakers" (working secular jobs) in 2008. With faithful hearts and focused vision, they have seen the church grow from close to 70 disciples in 2008 to a present membership of 115 disciples. This church is one of the fastest-growing underground churches in China, and it has raised up a strong campus ministry for the next generation of leaders. Last winter their Special Missions Contribution well exceeded their goal, and they made the decision to use the excess money to support other smaller underground church plantings nearby.

Even this year, Miki's goal is to go back to leading campus ministry despite her full schedule of family life, work, shepherding, and leading. This is Miki's heart, her example, her purposed vision being fulfilled—on this, her continuing pilgrimage in China. Her life embodies the spirit of Psalm 84:10:

> Better is one day in your courts
> than a thousand elsewhere;
> I would rather be a doorkeeper in the house of my God
> than dwell in the tents of the wicked.

CHAPTER THIRTEEN

The Canaanite Woman: Leadership and Boldness

Teresa Fontenot

Mathew 15:21-28; Mark 7:24-40

She had missed her opportunity before; it would not happen again. Jesus, the miracle-working rabbi, had healed and exorcised many from her region, but not her daughter. Now rumor had it that he had come near her hometown to have a secret retreat with his disciples. She was determined to find him. Yes, she was a Greek and a pagan whose ancestors had long been enemies of the Jews, but Jesus had a reputation for uncommon compassion and kindness. Maybe he would take pity on her.

She just couldn't bear to see her daughter suffer any longer from the demon's evil cruelty. Her daughter bore many scars from the demon's attempts to destroy her. The things that came out of her mouth—the shrieks, the curses, and the threats—were frightening and heartbreaking. Neither of them had slept through the night in years. They lived alone and had few friends. She could never leave her daughter alone. As a mother, she hurt to witness this evil transformation. She regretted ever worshipping her local gods and often blamed herself for this tragedy. They had no life to speak of, only a living nightmare that never ended.

She knew Jesus could heal her daughter and change everything. He had healed Gentiles before. She had seen the healed people who came back from Galilee rejoicing—diseases cured, demons gone—because of this man Jesus. All spirits submitted to his commands. He was more than a rabbi—he had to be the Messiah of the Jews. No, this was no ordinary man, and she would do whatever was necessary to receive his blessing.

Determined and desperate

There he was. This was her opportunity. In her desperation, she cried out. Hers was the cry of a beggar—"Have mercy on me"—but a beggar who recognized Jesus for who he was: "Lord, Son of David." She had to make her request specific—she wouldn't get another chance—so she shouted, "My daughter is suffering terribly from demon possession." There, she got it all out. What did it matter if she made a spectacle of herself? A woman never addressed a man in public and certainly didn't go screaming after a respected leader, but she didn't let this stop her. When Jesus paused and cocked his ear in her direction, she knew that he had heard her, noticed her. What she didn't know was that she was about to be tested by Jesus.

Testing, testing…

Her first test would be the silence of Jesus and the attitude his disciples displayed. When at first she could not reach Jesus, she clutched at the disciples' cloaks and begged for help. She imagined she could read their minds as they glared down at her, annoyance written all over their faces: *We traveled here specifically to get away from people like her! We're here to take a break from preaching and healing. We are exhausted, and so is Jesus. We deserve a break! And this woman is so pushy, it's embarrassing—it's a good thing Jesus is ignoring her. She just needs to get the hint and go away.*

The second test was the barrier of race; the disciples' contempt for her Canaanite blood was only thinly veiled as righteous prejudice, ordained by God: *This woman is a Canaanite, a corrupt race that should have been destroyed by Joshua centuries ago. This woman is not like us; she is not chosen.*

They marched over to Jesus and said, "Send her away, for she keeps crying out after us" (Matthew 15:23). When Jesus responded, "I was sent only to the lost sheep of Israel" (v. 24), the woman could see the disciples nodding their smug agreement. *It is good that Jesus is putting her in her place.*

Ignoring their disgust, she fell to her knees, looked up into Jesus' face, called him Lord and begged for his help. She refused to take a hint, or even a direct rebuff. She would not take no for an answer. She knew she was the wrong gender, the wrong race, and the wrong religion. She also knew that she could not heal her daughter by herself. Jesus was her only hope. She would beg and plead for their lives. What did she have to lose?

But Jesus had one more test for her. She would be insulted for her religion and her ancestry by the only man who could help her. Jesus looked at her and said, "It is not right to take the children's bread and toss it to their little dogs." She humbly nodded her agreement.

Jesus was saying hard things, but she sensed the compassion in his face and voice—in fact, the twinkle in his eye suggested he was teasing her as an older brother teases a beloved younger sister. After all, he did call her a "little dog," and not a savage or wild dog. She couldn't give up now that she had his attention. Jesus was her only hope. Baal was stone, and had no power to drive out demons; this Jesus, who somehow had access to the power of the Jewish God, could save her daughter—she just knew it. She would pass this test. Jesus saw her as a helpless puppy begging at the table. Jesus was right. That was exactly who she was. She agreed with him. But she was not asking for the whole loaf—"little crumbs" for a "little dog" would be sufficient. "Yes, Lord, she said, thinking quickly and bowing even lower, "but even the dogs eat the crumbs that fall from their masters' table" (v. 27). And then she waited. All she needed was a word from Jesus. Just the right word would change her daughter's life and future.

Gold medal faith

At last Jesus spoke, with amusement and affection in his voice: "Woman, you have great faith! Your request is granted" (v. 28). That was all she needed to hear—at last she'd gotten the "crumb" she had boldly pleaded for. Her nightmare was over. Jesus had given his word, and her daughter would be transformed. Now she must rush home and see this miracle!

Jesus could have healed her child immediately, but first he wanted to test her. He wanted to draw out the courage and faith that lay deep within her heart. In fact, her faith was more important to him than the healing that he offered her daughter. She emerged as the "gold medal Olympian" in the great test of faith, with the distinction of being the only woman to ever hear these words from Jesus: "Woman, you have great faith!" It is not easy to impress the Son of God, but the Canaanite woman did just that.

She had only a short encounter with Jesus, but this woman's boldness and faith brought light into dark places in her life, and no doubt into the lives of many others. In fact, we know that when Paul visited this region thirty years later, he was greeted by many disciples who knelt and prayed with him (Acts 21:2–5). Perhaps they all came to faith because a feisty, desperate Canaanite mother went looking for a new start, and she would not take *no* for an answer.

Boldness with humility

When we look up the definition of boldness, we find: "not hesitating or fearful in the face of actual or possible danger or rebuff; courageous and daring; beyond the usual limits of conventional thought or action; imaginative; striking or conspicuous to the eye."[19] We can see all these attributes in this Canaanite mother. She overcame any inclination to be shy, and was willing to risk shame or rejection. At the same time, she was not obnoxious, but humble. This is a hard balance to strike. She was able to express clearly and adamantly her request without being disrespectful or arrogant. Her desire for change made her relentless in pursuing Jesus, but her humility drove her to her knees in making the request. She overcame silence. Being ignored is one of the worst things we can experience. In the face of the disciples' unkindness and prejudice, she did not respond in kind.

As an unknown Gentile, this mother stood out from the rest. Her faith in Jesus' power made her tenacious. She allowed no obstacle to prevent her from seeing her faith rewarded. She was bold but not brash. She was clever but not controlling. She was humble but never hostile. Her faith stood out, and if we will follow in her footsteps, we too can catch the eye of Jesus.

- How would you define boldness? Are you a courageous person? How would you define humility? How can a person be bold *and* courageous and humble?
- Do you have the boldness of this mother in your relationship with God? How persistent are you in prayer?
- We see in this woman that great acts of boldness are often prompted by a concern for someone else. How can selfishness hinder our boldness?
- What part does boldness play in your relationships with your church members, friends, coworkers and family? Can you think of a situation where you failed to be bold when you should have been?
- When have you been most filled with boldness? What issue in your life would improve if you had more boldness?
- Fearfulness, negativity, cynicism, discouragement, cowardice, and pessimism are all opposites of boldness. How can you protect your heart from these feelings?

The Canaanite woman found healing for her daughter because of her boldness and faith. When we allow our faith to make us bold, God can use us in powerful ways to help other people. Let faith make you bold; let God use you to help people.

Insecurity and lack of confidence produce ineffective leadership. In contrast, reliance on God makes one bold and effective. Note: the first focus is on self, the other focus is on God "With my God I can" (Psalm 18:29).

—Gloria Baird, Los Angeles, California

I must be willing to speak to someone (or a group) because it will make a difference for them. Though surrounding circumstances may tempt me to hold back, boldness requires me to step out of my comfort zone.

—Sally Hooper, Dallas, Texas

Leaders who have the most impact are those who are not afraid to stand out—as going with the flow rarely gets the difficult things done. Dare to be different, but make sure your convictions are based on God's word, not just your opinions or emotions.

—Chris Fuqua, Los Angeles, California

When I pull myself together in order to share my faith, I want the other person to have the same opportunity to answer to God about his/her life that I had— because someone took the time and loved God enough to speak the truth to me.

—Lisa Schnell, Methuen, Massachusetts

To gain boldness I must understand that God has a mission for me and that he will be with me as I do my personal best. Determining to put aside my fear, I cling to 2 Timothy 2:15. To do this I need to be determined over and over again to sit at Jesus' feet like Mary; to plan, act, and be like Abigail and Deborah; to accept God's timing like Esther; and to love like Jesus loved.

—Gayle Boardman, Melbourne, Australia

PROFILE

Amira Okundi, Nairobi, Kenya: Boldness
by Joy Freeman, Illinois

As an adult with "real-life" challenges and responsibilities, it's easy to look at teenagers and think that their battles, challenges, and even their joys are light and simple. Yet the life of a teenager today, especially a teen who has chosen to follow Christ, is all but simple or trivial.

As I watch my teenage friend Amira Okundi mature in her life and in her discipleship, I see her become a fearless fighter, a young woman filled with passion, fighting the spiritual battle between this world and the things of God. She has one goal in mind: to be used by God and to be victorious through her faith. While we can read about teenagers in the Bible—young men and women like Joseph, Timothy, David, Mary, and the young men in the book of Daniel—and admire their spiritual valor, we can sometimes fail to realize that God is also crafting similar stories in the lives of the teenagers who are in our very presence.

Like Joseph in Egypt and Daniel in Babylon, Amira enters a "foreign land" every day: her school. As she walks the corridors, she is an ambassador for Christ, without any friends from church to walk alongside her. While other students focus on sex, drugs, and relationships, Amira focuses on pleasing God and obeying his word. With God's word as her standard, she chooses to forego popularity for righteousness—knowing that to stand apart often means to stand alone.

I have watched Amira fight for her faith while being pursued by boys who think her faith is just a fad. I watched from the sidelines her decision to attend her school prom alone because none of the boys in her school shared her convictions about God. And I have proudly listened to her dreams and her desire to see her classmates come to Christ.

Amira has a heart of gold, a relentless passion, and great vision to see her friends come to Christ. I admire the way she refuses to allow the things she sees around her to dictate the things she does or who she will become. Although she is young, the path she chooses is determined by her faith. She does not conform to the consensus opinion of her fellow teens—she charts her own path. For instance, she began a discussion group called "Phoenix"—a "for teens by teens" forum to discuss relevant issues for students. Each week they invite a panel of guest speakers to share about the things they faced when they were younger. Every week Amira works with a small group of teens to develop a topic, create the content to be covered, and to select and recruit guests. They then send messages to their Facebook group with the agenda that will be covered. Nothing like this has ever been done before in the Nairobi Christian Church. Amira did not let this uncharted territory stop her from fulfilling the vision God had put on her heart.

Amira's journey as a disciple is one that I truly admire, and I thank God for allowing me to witness her inspiring faith. Her pursuit of God takes her down a road that is sometimes rocky and unclear—yet it is a path she has chosen to keep walking. In a world where teenagers have so much access and exposure to the world, Amira has chosen God. Her boldness and faith are a great reminder to all who know her—teenagers and grandmothers alike—that God can use us all to accomplish his will. You don't have to be old to be used by God, and your circumstances don't have to be perfect—you just need vision and boldness.

CHAPTER FOURTEEN

Lydia: Leadership and Persuasion
Tammy Fleming
Acts 16:11-15, 39-40

Lydia was possibly her given name, or perhaps it was just a description based on the geographical region of Lydia, surrounding the city of Thyatira, where she was born.[20] We know that she was prayerful—like Cornelius in Acts 10, she was a Gentile who sought the one true Creator God actively, in the absence of any apostles or rabbis or disciples who could instruct her to do so. Were her Sabbath prayers, out there by the riverbank, the catalyst that sent the angel into Paul's dreams to call him to Macedonia? God noticed Cornelius' worship and sent angels to bring Peter to preach to him and his household. It seems God is doing something similar here, as Paul miraculously finds his way to Lydia.

Years ago, my husband and I helped to plant a church in Stockholm, Sweden, a nation where less than five percent of the population ever enters a church for any reason. Sometimes we wondered why God had sent us there—Stockholm is kind of an out-of-the-way place, not as large as some significant global cities like Mexico City or Istanbul or Jakarta. But one night at a devotional, a new Christian named Harriet stood up to read from a journal she had kept as a young girl. She read a defeated entry she had written at about the age of fourteen, where she had lamented, *I can't seem to find you, God, so you will have to find me.* God heard those prayers, and decades later, he sent a tiny group of Christians to Stockholm—God found Harriet.

Prayer works. Prayer is something that everyone can do. Prayer is arguably the hardest work in the world, as Satan uses every tool in his arsenal to keep us off our knees; and yet prayer remains the most powerful weapon we have, available to every single one of us at any moment of the day or night. We can pray out loud, or silently in our thoughts, and God hears. We can pray a long psalm, adding our spontaneous thoughts and petitions, or just one secret sentence, and God hears. It is always challenging to me, when I am fretting over some stubborn obstacle in my way that won't move (I have this box of papers I can't seem to find time to file away) or truly worried about a Goliath-sized giant in my path (my friend is dying of cancer), to discover that the reason I am fretting and worrying is that I have not been praying specifically and deeply.

Lydia was prosperous. She was a businesswoman who traded purple textiles (the area around Thyatira was known for purple dye, made either from shellfish or roots of plants). She took her local product, brought it to the big city, and had success. She had a big house, large enough to be able to accommodate not only the members of her own household (this most likely included her servants, and possibly her own children)[21] but also large enough to comfortably accommodate Paul and his companions—men not related to her—under the same roof, without embarrassment. Acts 16:40 suggests that her home quickly became the regular meeting place for the new church planting in Philippi. It's possible she was a widow, as there is no mention of a husband or man as the head of her household. For whatever reason, she alone made the decisions for her household at this point in her life. She chose to be generous and hospitable, inviting first the mission team, and then the growing Philippian church, to use her home. Until Lydia was met and baptized (presumably after just one conversation, as were most disciples in the book of Acts), no one, during their few days in Philippi, had offered Paul, Silas and Timothy a place to stay. She was the first to meet this need, and, at that point, the only one around who could do so.

Lydia was persuasive. The NIV says that Lydia "invited us to her home… and she persuaded us" (16:15). The same verse in the NASB sounds a bit stronger: "she urged us…and she prevailed upon us." How strong was Lydia's invitation of hospitality?

Very strong, it turns out. The Greek word translated "invited" in the NIV and "urged" in the NASB is translated elsewhere in the Bible as *begged, implored, exhorted, encouraged, pleaded, and appealed.*[22] In the other passages where it appears, the term carries a message of urgency, almost desperation. It's the word the legion of demons used when they were *begging* Jesus to send them into the herd of pigs and not into the abyss (Matthew 8:31); it's the word the crowd used to *implore* Jesus to allow them to touch the fringe of his cloak, as many as touched it were cured (Matthew 14:36); it's the same word, in the parable of the unmerciful servant, that his fellow slave uses when he falls to the ground and *urges*, "have patience with me and I will repay you" (Matthew 18:29). It's the word used to describe how John the Baptist, with many *urgings* or exhortations, preached the gospel to the people who came out to him in the wilderness (Luke 3:18); and it's the same word Paul used when he *implored* God to take away the thorn in his flesh (2 Corinthians 12:8).

The language Luke uses at the end of Acts 16:15—"and she persuaded us" (NIV) or "prevailed upon us" (NASB) is even stronger. The definition of this Greek word is "to employ force contrary to nature and right; to compel by employing force; to constrain one by entreaties."[23] This word shows up only one other time in the New Testament: when the resurrected Jesus appeared to two disciples on the road to Emmaus, their hearts burned within them as he opened the Scriptures to them, and "they urged him strongly" to stay with them (Luke 24:29).

So Lydia's persuasion of Paul and his party to stay at her house wasn't just a polite invitation. She employed force, contrary to nature and right, to get them to stay with her! This is what *persuasion* is.

It's interesting to note that Lydia, a minutes-old baby Christian, succeeded in persuading the mighty apostle Paul to do what she wanted. This is encouraging evidence that although women are called to be in a submissive role in certain relationships (women are called to submit to husbands; both men *and* women are called to submit to parents, "masters" or employers, political or civic authorities, and ordained church leaders), we don't have to be paralyzed or trapped in any of these relationships. There is usually a way to persuade a person who is in authority over us to listen, to reconsider—and thus to effect change. "Through patience a ruler can be persuaded, and a gentle tongue can break a bone" (Proverbs 25:15). Perhaps the "force, contrary to nature and right" in these situations is the force of gentle persistence—the way the gentle tongue of a dog licks repeatedly at the marrow of a bone, eroding it away, until the bone is hollow and breaks easily. Perhaps it's the prayer of the persistent widow (Luke 18:1–8). We all know that nagging to get what we want is annoying and unbecoming—this cannot be what God is suggesting to us here. Lydia didn't nag Paul, but she did succeed in convincing him to do what she wanted—something which was a great benefit to him as well.

What power is in our hands to persuade? In what situations is God expecting us to be persuasive? I think of some parents I know, who need to be persuaded to fall back in love with their teenage children. Their teens, at the moment, are behaving in a way that makes them difficult to love, but they still desperately need their parents' love and respect. I think of some sisters I know, who need to be persuaded to follow Matthew 18:15—to approach a particular person in church and let them know that there is a problem in the relationship, and that they feel sinned against. We have all known women who allow urgent conversations like this to go un-initiated for years . . . and as time ticks by, they stockpile evidence, which seems to support their right to nurture a bad attitude. (Or perhaps you've done this yourself!) Paul *persuaded* the two sisters, Euodia and Syntyche, who were having a problem to reconcile (Philippians 4:2)—he employs the same word here; he wanted the church to persuade these women to resolve their problem. Each one of us can persuade people to reconcile their differences. Persuade them to take a step of faith to love, to engage, to do what is right in the sight of God—today!

We can also persuade people to begin to study out the gospel message in the Bible. To seek God. To make a decision to live with Christ as Lord. In the Bible, we often see persuasion like this: Peter, persuading the crowd to believe in Jesus in Acts 2:40; Paul and Barnabas in Acts 14:22, persuading the disciples in Lystra, Iconium, and Antioch (and the Ephesians in 20:1) to remain faithful; Paul, in Ephesians 4:1, persuading the disciples there to walk in a manner worthy of the calling of Christ. It is good for us to be reminded that God considers it appropriate for us to be strongly persuasive—even with our own children, we must be persuasive. We can forget how relentlessly Satan is proselytizing, and can hang back to such a great degree that we miss crucial opportunities to teach our kids how to defend themselves against the darkness.

Lydia wasted no time in employing her gift of persuasiveness. She convinced the strong-willed Apostle Paul to accept her hospitality. She persuaded the members of her household to listen to the truth about Jesus, and they all became disciples! Her persuasive spirit brought salvation to her household, comfort to Paul, and a sense of unity to the new church in her hometown.

- How have seen your prayers (or other people's prayers) persuade God?
- What are some situations you see around you that call for urging and persuasive words? In these situations, what holds you back from being persuasive?
- Think of times when you have been persuasive with someone. What thoughts, convictions, and scriptures caused you to be persuasive?
- What would help you to become a more persuasive person toward people you encounter who need to find a relationship with Jesus? Toward those who need to find courage or need to overcome a particular sin?

Lydia's persuasiveness had far-reaching effects. Likewise, our persuasiveness can touch the lives of others in ways we may never fully understand. Our prayers can persuade God, and our convictions about his truth can produce in us an urgency to help many women find a relationship with him.

Ultimately, the power of persuasion is in God's word. In order to be persuasive leaders, we must continually be growing in our knowledge and awe of God's Word, and in our ability to share it humbly and with deep personal conviction.
—Mary Lou Craig, Boonton, New Jersey

Influence is our greatest motivator. If I had to choose between influence or authority, I would choose influence. Influence moves someone's heart, where authority may only produce an outward response.
—Virginia Lefler, Chicago, Illinois

The only one I am married to is my husband, not my opinions.
—Elexa Liu, Hong Kong, China

Helping someone to understand that you have their best interest at heart is a key to persuasion. Also, appeal to them through the Scriptures with great examples. Share personal experience.
—Sally Hooper, Dallas, Texas

My dad would repeatedly say, "Spaced repetition." This phrase became implanted in my mind. People are rarely persuaded by things they hear only one time. A diamond undergoes gentle pressure relentlessly applied before it becomes a diamond. If something is really important, we need to say it again and again—not nagging, but repeating.
—Jeanie Shaw, Burlington, Massachusetts

PROFILE

Susan, New Delhi, India: Persuasion

by Nadine Templer, New Delhi, India

Susan is a single woman in her fifties. She works as a nurse. In 2009 she was invited to the twentieth anniversary service of the New Delhi church, where she was very impressed by the love and commitment of the disciples. She was soon baptized. A few months later she got a transfer one hundred kilometers outside of Delhi to a small town called Simbhavli, in a neighboring state. Traveling one hundred kilometers (about sixty-two miles) in India entails riding for hours on rickety buses down pothole-ridden roads through monstrous traffic jams in sweltering heat. A lot of people would have decided it wasn't worth the effort to come to church anymore. Not Susan.

Susan is resilient and determined. She did not let the obstacles deter her. Like a lot of Indian women, she has had to face adversity in her life. What would seem like unsurmountable hurdles to some of us is just another challenge to be embraced for Susan and the millions of courageous women in India. Susan decided to make the most of her new situation. She was determined to keep coming to church, and to bring friends with her!

She would hire a twenty-seater van and drive her friends to church on Sunday all the way to Delhi. She paid for it with her own money, and she earns a modest income. She faithfully attends all the meetings of the Delhi church. And when she arrives at church, she is known for her ready smile and joyful attitude. Susan filled that van up with friends on a weekly basis. It took a lot of persuasion and boldness on her part, but she decided she would not take *no* for an answer. Week after week, with dogged determination and a winning attitude, Susan convinced her friends to attend church in Delhi. She did not stop there though.

Susan has a great heart filled with compassion. She came across a young teen, Salomi, who worked as a maid in someone's house. This young lady was being abused and mistreated. Susan rescued her and "adopted" her, and had the girl move in with her. Soon Salomi became a disciple.

Compelled by Christ's love, Susan has also started a local ministry in her town, seeking to persuade the women and men around her to turn to the love of Jesus. Women are not treated with much respect in India, yet Susan did not let that hold her back. Visitors started coming to her home to study the Bible. Susan would ask disciples from Delhi to travel all the way to her town to teach during the week. People started studying the Bible, and in the last couple of months, two of Susan's friends have been baptized, and several of her neighbors are studying the Bible. All alone in a new town, Susan has planted a church in a very challenging mission field!

Susan will be retiring in three years. At that point she will move back to her home state of Kerala in South India. Before she leaves Simbhavli, she prays to reach her goal: she wants to make her little church group sustainable. Susan's goal is to bring young people to Christ so they can keep the church going, growing, and thriving when she leaves that place.

Susan lives her genuine faith. She has made the most of her new life situation and has borne fruit from it, persuading others to follow Christ with her example and her enthusiasm. She is an inspiration to the whole church in a part of the world where women are not encouraged to stand out. Susan has not let the facts—that she lives in India, she does not have a lot of money, and she is single—hold her back. She lives out her convictions with an attitude of determination. She takes 2 Corinthians 5:14–15 seriously: "For Christ's love compels us, because we are convinced that one died for all, and therefore all died. And he died for all, that those who live should no longer live for themselves but for him who died for them and was raised again."

CHAPTER FIFTEEN

Miriam: Leadership and Initiative
Jeanie Shaw

Exodus 2:1–10

As Miriam sat on the Nile's bank, she filled her mind with stories of her nation's rich heritage and imagined its bleak future now that all the baby boys were being killed. Not being a mother, she could not fully understand the anguish she could so clearly see in her mother's eyes as she parted with her son. Her mother was a woman of faith, but things seemed a bit hopeless as she hid her precious young son in a waterproof papyrus basket among the river's reeds.

Doing what she could

Miriam couldn't bear to see her mother's tears, so she went down to the Nile where her baby brother was hidden. Perhaps, she thought, if she just showed up at this hiding place, she could think of something to do. Certainly, she thought God could do something to change this desperate situation.

Then it happened. Time seemed to slow as Miriam watched a royally dressed woman spot the basket where baby Moses lay, rocked to sleep by the gentle lapping of the water. Miriam watched her open the basket—and before Miriam could even think to hold her words inside, she was running over and proposing a seemingly outlandish idea to this beautiful Egyptian woman, whom she would soon recognize as Pharaoh's daughter. Miriam offered to bring a Hebrew woman (her mother, one of many whose breasts were full of milk) to nurse the boy for the woman. After the words came out of her mouth, she wondered if she had ruined everything by her boldness.

Instead, this initiative taken by Moses' older sister allowed God to unfold his plan for rescuing his people. Miriam had shown up, and she had opened her mouth. Although her plan might not have been well thought-out, she did something. She did what she could.

Taking a risk

Later in Miriam's life, we see this same type of bold initiative after the Israelites (through God's power and Moses' leadership) passed through the Red Sea on dry land:

> When Pharaoh's horses, chariots and horsemen went into the sea, the LORD brought the waters of the sea back over them, but the Israelites walked through the sea on dry ground. Then Miriam the prophetess, Aaron's sister, took a tambourine in her hand, and all the women followed her, with tambourines and dancing. Miriam sang to them:
>
> "Sing to the LORD,
>   for he is highly exalted.
> The horse and its rider
>   he has hurled into the sea."
> (Exodus 15:19–21)

Nobody told Miriam to take a tambourine and lead in singing. She simply moved forward and opened her mouth. All of the Israelite women followed her. She was leading them in song and praise to God and they all followed her.

Initiative is a necessary component of leadership. So often, lives aren't changed because no one wants to go where no one has been before. We worry, "What will people think?" or "What if I make a mistake?" Miriam took initiative in these two instances because she saw a need and because she was so full of gratitude to God. She had to do something. She was there.

Showing up

Showing up is key to becoming a spiritual leader. Do you hang back, thinking that someone else will do it or someone else will do it better than you? Are you an eager volunteer when a need presents itself? Do you walk on by, or do you inquire? Do you by faith "show up" to see how God can use you to help others? Are you one of the first ones to arrive at church or Bible discussion group and one of the last to leave because you are taking initiative with others? God calls us to take initiative, even if doing so does not come naturally to us. Godly leadership calls us to go beyond our comfort zone to give to others.

Taking initiative is godly. "For God so loved…that he gave" (John 3:16). He comes looking; he seeks us; he wants to bring the lost sheep back into the fold. Godly leadership takes initiative in response to God's love for us. "We love because he first loved us" (1 John 4:19).

If taking initiative is difficult for you, gain conviction from the Scriptures that "God did not give us a spirit of timidity, but a spirit of power, of love and of self-discipline" (2 Timothy 1:7). Watch others who do this well so you can learn from them. You can always encourage someone, share a scripture, offer to pray together. Try it. Even our smallest efforts mean more to others than we can know. When we initiate, God often uses us to reach into the heart of someone in need. We have God's Spirit living within us. As the children's song "This Little Light of Mine" says: "Hide it under a bushel—no!"[24] Let it shine.

After you initiate prayer with or for someone, you can follow up by asking how God is answering that prayer. Miriam's thought process seemed to include looking for solutions on how to make a situation better, even if it seemed hopeless. And years later, as her brother led the Israelites out of Egypt, she also overcame any inhibitions she might have felt to express her joyful and thankful heart for the encouragement of all.

Do you initiate greetings toward others, even when you don't know them? Do you ask questions so you can get to know them? This is part of taking initiative. It is one thing to answer and respond to others; that's being polite. Taking initiative means you engage others by showing them you care. Not only should leaders be quick to return calls and emails, but we should initiate relationships with others. Why? Because a godly leader cares about what is going on in the lives of others.

Hebrews 10 instructs us to consider (to think about ahead of time, mull over in our minds, pray about) how to spur each other on to love and good deeds:

> Let us hold unswervingly to the hope we profess, for he who promised is faithful. And let us consider how we may spur one another on toward love and good deeds. Let us not give up meeting together, as some are in the habit of doing, but let us encourage one another—and all the more as you see the Day approaching.
> (Hebrews 10:23–25)

Miriam's life teaches us another lesson, too—this one through a mistake she made. Her strength of taking initiative came with a corresponding weakness: pride. God taught Miriam that criticalness and self-importance are not part of godly leadership. She learned from this so that her strengths could continue to be used (see Numbers 12). We are all needed, but we are part of the body of Christ, and so we all need others in our life. In order to reflect the nature of Jesus, our humility should always go hand-in-hand with any initiative we take.

Getting feedback from others

Ask others around you if they see you as an initiator, or as one who holds back. Decide on one or two areas in which you can begin initiating. Talk to others whom you see as initiators; learn how they consider the needs of other people. Then show up. Consider the needs and say something; do something. There are always needs around you. God wants to use you.

Ask yourself the following questions to see how you are doing and how you can grow in taking initiative:

- Do you take initiative by showing up and engaging in fellowship opportunities?
- Do you hold back, waiting to be asked to fill a need, or do you identify needs and then do and say something so God can use you to help meet them?
- Do you initiate conversations, greetings, phone calls, questions?
- Do you consider how you can encourage others and stir them to love and good deeds?
- Do you initiate by showing gratitude and praise for God?

Miriam's initiative was crucial to Moses' survival. Moses was used by God to save a nation. Don't underestimate what God can do through you when you show up and speak up out of your love for God and concern for others.

Know your voice is needed. Certainly the church needs the voice of the men, but it also needs the voices and hearts of the women.
—Anita Allen, Hartford, Connecticut

Taking that first step forward is what a leader is called to do. You can always redirect that step, if you first make it.
—Teresa Fontenot, Sydney, Australia

Understanding that I am here for God's purposes helps me to understand that he needs for me to be ready and willing to act in any situation where I become aware of a need.
— Sally Hooper, Dallas, Texas

Leaders need to have a sense of direction as to where they are headed spiritually so they can guide others to grow in Christ and be their best. This takes planning, praying, and giving our talents and ideas. Initiate whatever is needed. A leader does not sit back and wait for others to start.
—Caron Vassallo, Melbourne, Australia

Some people come to church and are unhappy because "they didn't get anything out of it." If you come to church to give, you'll never be disappointed.
—Mary Bea Bouchet, Manassas, Virginia

Remember how you feel when you are remembered. Sometimes it's the little things you initiate—a text, a call, a saved seat, a birthday card, a thank you note, or letting someone know you are praying for or thinking of them—that are just what someone needs.
—Jeanie Shaw, Burlington, Massachusetts

PROFILE

Nadya Terzayn, Vinnytsia, Ukraine: Initiative

by Lena Wooten, Kiev, Ukraine

What do you do when you feel alone? Do you wait for someone else to organize something, or do you regretfully wish your situation was different, or do you seek to do what you can to impact your situation for good? Nadya Terzayn has chosen to step out on faith and watch God work through her life.

Nadya grew up in Ukraine. Her family was part of a small church there, consisting of approximately one hundred people. Nadya's parents had become Christians and she was the oldest child in her family and among all the families in the church. She was the first and only preteen in her church—and then became the first teenager in the church. She had no spiritually-minded peers around her, and no teen ministry. She could have felt sorry for herself and wished to live in other places, or she could have made excuses to keep from following Jesus—after all, she was the only one her age.

However, Nadya loved the church—and more importantly, she loved her God. She studied music as a young teen and brought her two fellow violin classmates to church with her. They were thirteen years old. She did not let the fact there was no teen ministry stop her from reaching out and building a teen ministry. She took initiative to "bring her own group." As Nadya grew and began to study the Bible, she made Jesus Lord and was baptized. Her fellow violinists, who had been coming to church with her, continued to come. Soon they all became disciples. Nadya's younger sister and younger brother also became disciples.

Nadya, beginning as the only one in her teen ministry, did not let her lack of resources slow her down. She had God, and she had faith in him. That was enough. If Nadya had not taken initiative, even as a young teen, she would likely still be alone—and her friends would have missed out on the love of God and his church.

Nadya didn't stop there. Knowing that she and her friends needed to be connected to other young people who were following Jesus, she organized ways for them to go to conferences and church youth camps in larger cities. She and the other teen disciples also became friends with a teen who is confined to a wheelchair and another who had cancer. Through their love, these two young people became Christians. Nadya's initiatives continued to have great impact—eternal impact.

After graduating from college, Nadya took a job with a television production company. However, she wanted to learn more as a disciple and train to be more effective in her leadership. She enrolled in the Kiev School of Missions and planned to be part of a three-year training program there.

After she'd been part of the training program for three months, a need arose for leadership in a small Ukrainian church of about thirty disciples. The church had lost its leaders and they were in need. Nadya, now twenty-four years old and having just begun her training, was asked if she would like to go (along with a brother whom she did not really know) to lead the ministry in the Vinnytsia church. Nadya's faith-inspired initiative throughout her teen years had been preparing her for yet another step of faith. Nadya is now living and leading in this new situation and is continuing to grow and to impact others.

Four disciples in the church in Vinnytsia are deaf. Many of their deaf friends have wanted to study the Bible. Nadya continues to overcome challenges, learning sign language so that she can study the Bible with the deaf community. God is blessing her initiative as her life impacts others for eternity.

CHAPTER SIXTEEN

Deborah: Leadership and Inspiration
Teresa Fontenot
Judges 4 and 5

Deborah, wife of Lappidoth, sat once more under the tree in the hills to judge legal disputes among her people. She knew that God spoke through her more than any other person in Israel, male or female, but still, she bore a weighty responsibility. Nevertheless, if she listened to his voice, she had peace and confidence that she was making right judgments. Deborah was unique as the only woman to ever be given the honor of leading God's people. Her prophecies had always come true, and even she could not fail to recognize that God spoke through her. Since most of God's people could not read God's words for themselves, Deborah realized the significance of being the "mouthpiece" of God. She was both honored and humbled by her role as the prophetess-judge of Israel. Deborah was not an avoider of conflict; in fact, her days were filled with it. Solving problems was her life. As she sat under the tree, her heart was moved again to bring unity and peace to her people. Her "mother's heart" wanted the Israelites to live in peace, loving God and one another in perfect harmony. Together with a God of justice and righteousness, she would do whatever she could to bring this about.

Twenty years had passed since her people had done evil in God's eyes, and many family members had been taken by the Canaanites as slaves. She could remember, along with so many others, those terrible days when the enemy had come into their homes, dragged off their children, and killed their husbands and fathers. The Israelites who had escaped with their lives were left devastated. The weeping and wailing could be heard for miles around. Canaanites hated Israelites and they were cruel. The sufferings of Deborah's people were a continuous ache in her heart. They had lived with this reality and sadness now for twenty years. Some could not even remember what life had been like before. But Deborah sensed that the hearts of her people were softening—the bitterness and anger were beginning to give way to repentance. As God spoke through her, his people were beginning to listen again. They were turning their hearts back toward God, taking responsibility and crying out for mercy instead of justice. God's children, the ones Deborah had adopted, were once again honoring and serving the LORD. With one voice, they "cried to the LORD for help" (Judges 4:3).

Inspiration, not hesitation

Finally, the LORD had given Deborah a message of deliverance. He would lure Jabin's military commander, Sisera, into their hands. Victory and reconciliation would at long last be theirs. Deborah was bursting with joy and anticipation. There was no time to waste—she would tell Barak this great news immediately. Barak was hesitant, but she understood. Although he was a courageous military commander, Barak did not have the direct line of communication to God that was so obvious with Deborah. He did not doubt God or Deborah, but he did have some doubt as to whether he could carry out God's plan without her. Barak trusted Deborah's faith more than his own. She was special. Even so, Deborah gave him a mild reproof for his faithless response, telling him that a woman would win this battle. Barak accepted this. He was not fighting for his own glory; he just wanted the assurance of having a prophet at his side, to help him and his men feel confident that victory would soon be theirs.

Although Deborah was much more comfortable bringing justice through words, she was willing to take up a sword, if that's what it took. She did not hesitate. Deborah was a wife, judge, prophetess, leader, motivator, deliverer, protector, and a warrior for God. She would fight and trust God, even though some of her people refused to join them. Deborah knew what God wanted and she was fiercely determined. Although putting herself in the front of this great battle was not her idea, she had to admit that watching God's miracle unfold was astounding.

Barak had organized the ten thousand men just as God instructed. He was a strong leader, forceful in battle, but going up against the enemy's nine hundred iron chariots was daunting. The Israelites could easily be mowed down by these tank-like weapons. Of course the odds were against them—that is how God likes it! He loves to overpower the strong with the weak. After all, God had helped Joshua defeat a king called Jabin from Hazor when the odds were against him as well. Deborah had no doubt that God would be working behind the scenes.

As Corrie ten Boom once wrote, "When a train goes through a tunnel and it gets dark, you don't throw away the ticket and jump off. You sit still and trust the engineer." This was God's specialty. He wanted everyone to know that he alone brings the victory, and he alone should receive the glory.

God caused a panic. He opened the heavens, as only he can. The rain poured, the earth shook, the river overflowed, and the heavy iron chariots sank in the mud. The Canaanites had trusted in their superior weaponry, and now they were stuck. God's people were high and dry . . . and it was a good thing. God won the battle, and the Israelites swooped in to finish it off. Jael "nailed" the Canaanites' powerful military commander, Sisera, when he deserted his troops and ran away on foot. Jael, acting as God's "secret weapon," dealt the decisive blow for Israel's victory. This is how *God* defeats his enemies.

Inspiration and praise

Deborah, Barak, and all the people of God were bursting with joy. The cruel, oppressive Canaanites were defeated. Family members were reunited. The nightmare of slavery was over. They could hardly believe the power and the mercy of their mighty God. It was time to sing!

Deborah loved music and singing. Songs enabled her to express the deepest and most heartfelt of emotions. This amazing victory had to be recorded. Deborah was a praiser. Her bond with God filled her heart with awe. There was truly no one like their God. After all, it was her habit of exalting God that caused his courage to flow through her. She must sing about it with Barak before the people, and they must hear the story so it could be passed on. Deborah knew that we remember so much more when we put it to music. She would recount all of God's deeds in song, and he would be enthroned in her praise. Her people would hum this tune as they worked and played, never forgetting the lessons in it. Deborah was an exceptionally gifted woman who filled many roles, but when describing herself, she sang that she "arose a mother in Israel" (Judges 5:7). She saw herself as the protector of her people, standing as the link between them and the LORD. Finally, harmony and peace had come to God's people. Deborah felt privileged to lead at this time in history as she saw God's enemies perish and the people who loved him become "like the sun when it rises in its strength" (Judges 5:31).

Inspiration, the breath of life

One lesser-used definition of the word *inspiration* is *breathing*—specifically, the act of inhaling. While others were breathing in the threats of the enemy, Deborah was breathing in the words and power of God. She had a close communion with God, and her life was filled with an awe of him. Because her

God was so big, she did not hesitate to do as he said. Bold confidence flowed from her prayer life. Her consistent praise and honor of God was the secret to her fighting spirit and her compassionate heart. Her mind was filled with God's thoughts and ways as she led the people.

Inspiration cannot come to people whose God is "too small." How big is your God? Do you spend time praising and meditating on his power and character? Paul's greatest ambition in life was "to know Christ" (Philippians 3:10). Although Deborah fulfilled many roles in her busy life, *knowing* God and *following* God were at her core.

Inspiration also means breathing life *into* something. Even strong men were inspired by Deborah's absolute trust in a never-failing God. People wanted to follow her and listen to her. We are drawn to people who calm our fears and revive our faith by their unwavering certainty in God. Deborah believed God's words enough to put them into action. Inspiration is believing and acting despite the obstacles. Deborah knew the problems, but was not dissuaded. She even included them in her song. Through this, we can see what inspiration is *not*. Inspiration is not *self-absorbed*; it does not indulge in "much searching of heart," as the indecisive tribe of Reuben did (Judges 5:16); it does not *hesitate*—it does not "linger by the ships," like the Danites (v. 17); and it is not *safe*—tucked away in coves, like Asher (v. 17). Inspiration is when the leaders "take the lead" and "the people willingly offer themselves" (v. 1). Inspiration shatters despair, doubt, and anxiety. Inspiration is filled with joy and "re-joy." Inspiration gives us excellent wisdom and abundant spiritual energy. Inspiration is when *all* things point to God.

It is no small thing to God when we are no longer inspired by him. Jeremiah 2:19 says,

> " 'Consider then and realize
> how evil and bitter it is for you
> when you forsake the LORD your God
> and have no awe of me,' declares the Lord, the LORD Almighty."

Being inspired, or "breathed into" by God can only come from our time spent with him. The fact that Deborah walked closely with God is reflected in her life. As the moon reflects the light of the sun, we can only reflect God's greatness as we absorb his light. Consider the following questions to help you grow in your inspiration:

- Does your study of God's word inspire awe in you? If not, what can you do to change this?
- Do you pray with awe and wonder as you ask God to do great things? Do you take time to praise him for the many ways he is working "behind the scenes" for you and for others?
- Are you a "doer of the word"? We all have varying abilities, but *anyone* can obey, and God promises that you will be blessed in all you do (James 1:22, 25).
- Do you share the wonder of God's mighty acts in your life, in the lives of those around you, and in the lives of heroes in the Bible? Consider writing your own poem, song or story to remember some of the great deeds of God.
- When you lead others, do you inspire greater faith in the people you lead? Do you see the "people willingly offer themselves" as you take the lead?
- Identify one *uninspiring* aspect of your life you can "throw off," and another *inspiring* quality you can "put on." How can you develop that characteristic?

Like Deborah, let us inspire others with our faith, our courage, and even our songs:

> "When the princes in Israel take the lead,
> when the people willingly offer themselves—
> praise the LORD!" (Judges 5:1)

Thankfully, inspiration does not necessarily mean charisma, although we can always be growing in our communication skills. A person's life and obvious convictions are powerful means of inspiration (Hebrews 11) and are a necessary part of effective leadership.
—Mary Lou Craig, Boonton, New Jersey

Inspiration is not just about speaking or preaching in a public setting. Inspiration is found in the life that you live.
—Sally Hooper, Dallas, Texas

We underestimate the need for inspiration. I always think of Miriam, as she led the women with singing and tambourines after they walked across the parted Red Sea. The Bible says, "All the women followed her" (Exodus 15:20). One of the greatest things we can do for our women is to inspire them—with God's love, with God's great purposes for their lives, with a great vision of faith and the power of God. My heart has always responded best to inspiration rather than scolding.
—Geri Laing, Lake Worth, Florida

As I observe nature, I am inspired by God's greatness, attention to detail, and creativity. I am inspired by individuals as I watch them overcome weaknesses and step out on faith. Sometimes we just need to pause and take note of things around us in order to be inspired.
—Jeanie Shaw, Burlington, Massachusetts

PROFILE

Mariana Suiu, Bucharest, Romania: Inspiration
by Jeanie Shaw, Massachusetts

Mariana was about five years old when we met. I stepped into her world, which was confined to a dilapidated cinder block orphanage in Bucharest, Romania. She owned nothing and she had no family. She was an orphan.

I was there on behalf of a benevolent organization, HOPE *worldwide*, to begin a program celebrating children's birthdays. That may seem a rather simple beginning, but the children in Mariana's orphanage never celebrated birthdays. They did not know when they were born, as no one had ever really cared enough to write it down—and certainly their birthdays had never been celebrated. Orphans were not valued. The future for an orphan was not bright or visionary. Orphans in the school system were rarely even offered the chance to take a test to enter high school. They were considered inadequate. Few went to high school; most ended up on the streets. Not only did Mariana grow up without a family, but she was also physically challenged. Mariana is a little person—a dwarf. Life's circumstances were challenging for her.

As I got to know the children I was drawn to Mariana's tender heart and genuine smile. Her compassionate heart was evident. Many stray dogs roamed the streets around the building. Most people hated these strays and considered them a public nuisance. But Mariana befriended them and tried her best to care for them. She loved them deeply. Perhaps she felt a certain kinship to their plight. As I visited several times each year, Mariana became a special friend to me. She was also like a sister to Jacob, our son, who joined our family when he was twelve. He and Mariana grew up together inside the orphanage in Bucharest, enduring many difficulties along the way.

Mariana came to live in a home opened by HOPE *worldwide*, and was drawn to the love she began to receive there. Over time, she came to realize that this love came from God, and she gained a vision to make her life count.

Mariana began visiting the church in Bucharest, and after learning of God's love and grace, she became a disciple of Jesus. As she began to grasp God's view of her—the value and purpose he saw in her life—she became more and more confident. She came to believe that God sees her as his beautiful and valuable daughter. She was now a daughter of the King of kings.

For a while, Mariana lived with an older woman in the church, who graciously took her in. Through challenging times, Mariana grew as a disciple and as a young woman of deep character. She graduated high school and did what most would have deemed impossible—she entered the university. Never having lost her love for animals, in 2013 she graduated from veterinarian school. Not only does she help animals, but Mariana is actively involved in something even more important: helping others know the love of her God. Although she is short in physical stature, Mariana is tall in love for God and for people. She has not allowed her most challenging circumstances to dull her vision for what God has called her to be and to do.

Mariana says, "Living as a disciple is not easy, but it's the most beautiful life. As you look back and as you look toward your future, you know that God has written your story. He also knows when this story is over—when his mission with you is complete.

"I have learned deep thoughts from God's word—as if he whispers in my ears. I still have not learned enough. God has much constant love for us that can inspire us to live victoriously in him till the end of our life.

"This year it will be my tenth year in the Kingdom. I want to do my best from one year to the next—with the vision to help others to love God. I believe he has put something special in me to attract people to him."

CHAPTER SEVENTEEN

Mary of Bethany: Leadership that Doesn't Burn Out
Jeanie Shaw

Luke 10:38–42; John 11:1–45; 12:1–8

Jesus passed through Bethany many times during his years of ministry. The siblings Mary, Martha, and Lazarus had befriended him, and they always enjoyed their visits together. How Mary treasured the memory of those times! She recounted the unimaginable miracles she had witnessed. Her own brother had been raised from the dead, and her dear friend and lord had recently been crucified, only to resurrect three days later. The sacrificial love and magnificent power she had known from Jesus still burned in her heart, even though he was gone. Because it remained burning in her heart, she was determined not to "burn out" in her love and service to him. She possessed a relationship with Jesus that kept their friendship alive throughout his lifetime, and would now allow her to experience a peace that would keep her going through her hard times of confusion and loss.

All too often, leaders start off eager to serve and then become overwhelmed with the cares of life—weighed down by their own concerns, and others'. What enabled Mary to keep her love for Jesus so fresh that she exhibited extravagant love even at the end of Jesus' life, when it was becoming dangerous even to be Jesus' friend?

She was often at the feet of Jesus.

Three times we find Mary at the feet of Jesus:

- **She listened at his feet (Luke 10:38–42).** Mary could often be found sitting at the feet of Jesus, savoring his words as precious morsels—words that breathed life into her soul and directed her steps throughout the day. How often do we take the needed time to simply listen to Jesus' words?

Mary sat and listened to Jesus while her sister was busy doing acts of service. As leaders, there are always many things to do and many people to care about. Are we so busy *doing* (even when our *doing* is serving) that we don't take time to be still before Jesus? We will be sure to "burn out" or run out of fuel if we don't consistently take his words into our hearts.

- **She fell at his feet, showing her desperate need for his help (John 11:32).** When Mary's brother died, she ran to find Jesus, and fell at his feet in sorrow and desperation. What does desperation for Jesus look like for you? Mary was heartbroken because of her brother's death. Mary could have looked Jesus in the eyes and asked him why he had not arrived in time to heal her brother . . . but Jesus was not only her friend, he was also her lord. She was humble before him even as she was desperate for his compassion, his strength, and his power. When we don't fall at Jesus' feet with our burdens, they soon become too heavy and overwhelming for us to carry.

- **She showed extravagant love at his feet (John 12:1–8).** Mary honored Jesus by anointing his feet. This act went beyond the customary "honoring"—which consisted of anointing someone's head—by pouring expensive ointment on his feet and unbinding her hair (an act that was not considered "proper" for a Jewish woman to perform in public). Mary took perfume, likely the most precious thing she possessed, and spent it all on Jesus. She then wiped his feet with her hair. Although this extravagant expression was criticized by some, Mary did not hesitate to break the expensive jar of spikenard. Love does not worry about the cost. It gives all, and only regrets that it has not still more to give. When we love extravagantly, we don't continue doing what we do merely out of duty—it wells up from within our hearts. While we must often rely on obedience (which is good and right), if we aren't motivated by extravagant love, we will tire of duty.

She was honest, vulnerable, and expressive.

Mary was not afraid to cry or express her grief. After her brother's death, she fell at Jesus' feet, weeping. Her tears moved Jesus so much that he also began to weep. Are we afraid to share our emotions with Jesus?

Mary even expressed her disappointment with Jesus for "letting" her brother die. Too often, we burn out because we hold in our feelings. When we are not honest about the emotions we carry, and don't take them to Jesus, we become anxious and overwhelmed. Because Mary knew where to take her emotions, she also didn't get distressed when her sister, Martha, criticized her in front of Jesus (Luke 10:38–42). Mary was secure in her own skin. When we emotionally react to critique (especially when someone criticizes us in front of someone whose opinion is important to us) we can also become tempted to quit relationships. This will also quickly cause burnout.

Mary spent time with her family.

Family was valuable to Mary. We know this because of the love they shared and the way they are spoken of as a group. Mary felt great sadness when she (temporarily) lost her brother. Together, the siblings (who were probably not married) shared a common faith and practiced hospitality. God puts us in families for a reason, and too often we neglect the refreshment that home can provide. While not all family situations are refreshing or helpful in serving Jesus, when they are, we need to enjoy the joy and comfort they bring. They can be a haven in the storm. Families are not only intended to provide companionship, but also to make us stronger as we serve and practice hospitality together. Leaders can tend to spend so much time concerned with others outside their family that they miss out on the refreshment God provides through their families. When we neglect time with our family, we become a weaker link, less able to carry the loads that leadership demands.

Mary chose what was best as compared with what was just "okay."

Mary's sister Martha's "claim to fame" was her propensity to be busy—too busy. Martha complained to Jesus that Mary was not helping her with the preparations when Jesus and his disciples came for a visit. Jesus made it clear to Martha (and all of us) that Mary's posture of sitting at Jesus' feet—listening to his words—was the better choice. If Martha continued in her pattern of continually giving without receiving, she would surely have become even more resentful, and eventually her spiritual batteries would have run out. Perhaps Mary was tempted to join Martha in the preparations—we don't know. However, we do know that Mary's choice to be filled with Jesus' teaching was the best one. We always have choices for how we spend our time. For many of us, it often feels more important to get our surroundings in order than it is to get our hearts in order. We must remember that we can choose our priorities.

Our circumstances in life change over time. Our workload, the number of children we have, our health, and our emotional strength will all change throughout different stages of our lives. The years before we have children and after our children leave the nest are times when our capacity to spread our service and influence often increases. At other times—for example, during times when we are not healthy—we can't carry as much as our healthy sisters can carry. Circumstances can dictate our available time, and we must choose and prioritize with wisdom and biblical priorities. We also need to take care of our bodies. As my husband often says, "We only have one horse to ride, so take care of your horse." Although God calls on us to make the most of the time we have (Ephesians 5:15–16), sometimes we can be guilty of trying to do more than we are physically able to do. We would do well to ask for help in evaluating what is best. When "doing what we can" combines with God's power, our contribution is always enough. Yes, Mary technically could have "done more" by helping Martha with all the preparations, but she chose what was best. Perhaps she understood that if she did not *first* sit at Jesus' feet, she would not *later* be able to do much else. Spiritual leaders begin with the most important priorities, and then do what they can—no more and no less.

It is so tempting to choose the "urgent" over the important—laundry over the Bible, or e-mail over prayer—but a wise woman will live purposefully as she chooses her priorities each day. Talk with others about correctly ordering the priorities in your life. Like Mary, I hope you will learn to choose what is best. The choices we make will determine our ability to keep serving Jesus throughout our entire lives.

- Do you sit first with Jesus, or wait until after the "most urgent" things are done?
- Is Jesus simply a great teacher to you, or are you utterly dependent on him for your daily walk? What does dependence on Jesus look like for you?
- Do you love with a "reckless abandon" or with calculated response?
- Are you often tempted to "do" before you spend time at the feet of Jesus? If so, what one decision can you make to change this pattern and choose what is best?
- Do you draw refreshment from your family, and give refreshment to your family?
- In your current season of life, what does choosing the best priorities look like?

Mary's life touched many others. Her life left a legacy that inspires us even today. Like Mary, let us sit at Jesus' feet, speak honestly and vulnerably, gain strength from our families, and choose what is best. As the writer of Hebrews also encourages us, "Consider him…so that you will not grow weary or lose heart" (Hebrews 12:3).

The only way to make it to the finish is to walk step by step with God—and to continually let his word shine his light on every step of that pathway. In order to not be left empty, we have to let him fill us. He provides our daily manna.

—Gloria Baird, Los Angeles, California

Go back to the cross. Remember your sin. Then you will be reminded why you do what you do.

—Teresa Fontenot, Sydney, Australia

I used to assume that leaders lead because they love helping others. I have found that it is not always the case. Some are driven to sacrifice for God; others to give back because of gratitude for what they have been given. I am sure there are many more reasons. Whatever the motivation, leaders have to make time for "self-care." Why? Because burning out happens over time, and once you have reached that point it is very hard to continue leading with joy and vision. Preventative medicine in needed. As Grandma used to say, "An ounce of prevention is worth a pound of cure."

—Karen Louis, Singapore

Close relationships are the antidote to burnout. If you start doing the work of Jesus without close relationships, look out. A close friend with whom you share anything and everything will help protect you and keep you refreshed.

—Virginia Lefler, Chicago, Illinois

You can't do everything and help everybody—but God can. He will do what we cannot. Pray and give them over to God, who loves them more than we ever could. Also, don't forget to let others know when you need to be ministered to. They can't read your mind.

—Jeanie Shaw, Burlington, Massachusetts

PROFILE

Norah Namei, Kigala, Rwanda: Leadership that Doesn't Burn Out

by Norah Namei

My story begins in 1998, when I was baptized as a disciple while in my second year at a university. I immediately began to dream about joining the full-time ministry, as I always wanted more time to study the Bible with people and teach them about following Jesus. My prayer was answered after eleven years of prayer and fasting.

I come from a family of staunch Anglicans—my dad and brother are reverends, and my two sisters are married to reverends. Given this background, they were against my decision to become a disciple. And when I gave up my job as an administrator in a theological college to join the ministry, my family had mixed feelings—they thought I was just going to sit home as a minister's wife. Over time, they have come to appreciate what we are doing on the mission in Kigali, Rwanda, and they always pray and encourage us to keep up the good work we are doing.

My husband and I are Ugandans working as missionaries in Rwanda. We were barely one year in marriage when we were called into full-time ministry. We were very excited about the news, and immediately prepared to go to Nairobi, Kenya, for further training. I was two months pregnant with our first baby, and during the first few months of our stay in Nairobi I was always sick. Adjusting to being pregnant for a first time, living in a new country, being newly married, and working in a new job was a challenge for me (and my husband). We prayed together often and sought advice whenever we faced challenges. I had to learn to rely on God, and to focus on relationships and not results. Mature Christian friends helped me to understand that deepening my relationship with God was key to success in the ministry.

In 2010, we were sent to work with the church in Kigali, Rwanda. I was both excited and anxious about what to expect on the mission. The first three years were very difficult. We dealt with culture shock because the people and their culture were so different. Rwanda endured genocide in 1994, and this has greatly affected the people's lives. Many have to deal with issues of trust and forgiveness. This affects the church in terms of coming together, learning to have deep and meaningful relationships, and in being willing to open up their hearts. In their culture, being vulnerable is a weakness. This tempts them to be "religious on the outside." It makes it difficult to reach the heart and provide the real spiritual help needed for growth. This requires much love and patience. The church was small, and in order to help make the singing and worship more encouraging, I learned how to drum, and I began serving as the drummer whenever there was no brother available. Another challenge was the language—for a while, we relied on translators.

We had to work so hard to learn the language, and we thank God that now we can communicate without waiting on someone to translate. My husband and I are currently studying the Bible with numerous people deep in the village (in their local language), and all of them want to be baptized!

There is overwhelming poverty here, yet people are eager to learn about God. Many families eat one meal a day and have never slept on a mattress. Many walk for four hours to and from church, in order to come and listen to God's word. Christians from other congregations have sent money to buy mattresses and blankets for the disciples here. Our church was overwhelmed with joy upon receiving the blankets and mattresses.

We often wanted to quit the mission in Rwanda because of the many challenges we have faced, but we have decided to persevere and not give up. It has taken a lot of prayers, tears, and fasting for us to continue moving, and we praise God for the work he is doing. Please keep on praying for us.

CHAPTER EIGHTEEN

Bithiah, Pharaoh's Daughter: Leadership and Helping the Poor

Nadine Templer

Exodus 2:1–10

A richly robed young woman walks by the river bank and hears a baby cry. She goes over to take a look and soon realizes that this is one of the Hebrew babies condemned to death. She chooses to act, and out of the goodness of her heart, she decides on the spot to adopt him.

"From everyone who has been given much..."

The Bible says, "From everyone who has been given much, much will be demanded" (Luke 12:48). Centuries before Jesus uttered those words, Pharaoh's daughter understood them. She was likely named Bithiah, which means "daughter of Yah" or Yahweh (1 Chronicles 4:18; she was the wife of Mered, also referred to in the Jewish Midrash as the adoptive mother of Moses). Bithiah realized that her privileged position came with a responsibility. Just like the Samaritan in Luke 10, she responded and did not walk away when she encountered a need. Bithiah knew she had much to give. She realized that her royal position gave her the ability to reach out and share. In a world of "haves" and "have-nots," Pharoah's daughter knew where she stood. She was a leader because she used her position to make a difference.

If you are reading this book, you are most likely in that first category also—the "haves." We have been given much. What are we going to do about it? How are we handling that responsibility?

Bithiah was keenly aware of her role. Like the "good Samaritan," she was also observant, on the lookout for needs. She knew about the suffering of the Jews. She knew she could not save all of them. But she could do something (Mark 14:8). Bithiah obviously was prepared to respond the way she did. It is something she must have thought about. Do we pray and prepare ourselves spiritually to respond to the needs of the less fortunate?

Bithiah did not walk away. How many times have we walked away from a beggar or a documentary or a Facebook post about the poor and felt guilty for not responding? Often we walk away not because we have a bad heart, but perhaps because we are not prepared.

Pharaoh's daughter Bithiah showed leadership by responding and acting on the spot. She was bold and quick. She was a leader, not because she was Pharaoh's daughter and had a royal title, but because she stepped forward and rose to the occasion when the opportunity came.

"She felt sorry"

Bithiah responded from the heart. When she saw baby Moses in his basket, abandoned and with no mother, she reacted with the compassion and care a mother would feel. At that moment she was not a royal princess—she was a woman with a big heart. The Bible tells us that she "felt sorry for him" (Exodus 2:6). At the sight of the helpless little baby, her heart melted.

She did not hesitate; she did not spend ages contemplating and wondering whether she could handle it, whether this was the right thing to do. She knew. She reached out and took a risk. This was a Hebrew baby and she was well aware of that. She knew the dangers associated with a royal princess adopting a Hebrew baby. She suspected it would not be the most popular step she had ever taken. Indeed, if Jewish tradition is true, this act likely led to her eventual exile from Pharaoh's court and her marriage to a Jew named Mered.

She went with her heart and stepped out in faith. Her compassion was bigger than the possible risk. She ended up raising one of the most powerful men the world has ever known.

Bithiah was a kind person—open, and willing to interact with people from a lower social standing. She asked advice from Miriam, the baby's sister. As a result, God's plan was enabled.

When we see a need, when we encounter poverty, when we witness injustice, do we step out in faith, or do we hesitate, calculating all the risks, often ending up not doing what our heart tells us? Have we hardened ourselves to the cries of the orphans and the poor, rationalizing and waiting for someone else to take care of things?

The question we should ask ourselves is not "why?" but rather "why not?"

She adopted him

It says in Exodus 2:10 that "he became her son." She did not simply give him something to eat or pay for his education, even though those would have been kind and noble gestures. She actually went all the way and made him her son. She broke all the barriers and took into her family the child of another woman, gave him a name, and raised him as her own.

She did not have to do this. But she did it anyway. This was about doing the best for the child, not herself. She gave Moses a meaningful name and not surprisingly, he grew into a fine man, a leader who would change Israel's destiny.

Helping the poor out of love and not compulsion is what God wants us to do. God adopted us as his own. He even sacrificed his own child for us. When we adopt children, we are imitating God (Ephesians 1:5; 5:1). It is the most beautiful story of redemption, and we get to be a part of it. How blessed are adoptive parents!

People always say how "lucky" adopted children are. Actually the "lucky" or blessed ones are the adoptive parents. They get an understanding of God that is hard to grasp any other way. My husband and I have had the privilege of adopting two little Indian girls, and they have changed our lives! Our daughters Esther Sonali and Priscilla Mercy are precious beyond measure, and are growing into amazing young women of God.

Adoption may not be the right path for every family, but we are all called to have compassion and to serve the poor. And if we are spiritual leaders, God calls us to follow Jesus' example of seeing needs and finding ways to meet them. We see God's heart through Jesus as he noticed the poor, fed them, touched them, and cared for them as he lived his life each day. Spiritual leaders strive to have the heart of God as they learn from him and rely on his Spirit. Like Bithiah, we can make a difference in many lives, just by helping one.

- Take time in your day to think of and pray for the poor and needy. What are specific ways you can serve them?
- When other people initiate serving the poor, are you eager to join in, or do you often consider yourself too busy to help?
- How does serving the poor change our character?

Each of us is only one person, but out of our privilege, we need to share and extend a hand. Pharaoh's daughter was a leader among women. She was kind, compassionate, and generous, and she took a step of faith without concern for the risks to herself. Let us imitate her faith and use our privileged position to reach out to the less fortunate. Let us do so because it is the right thing to do, but who knows…there may be a Moses or an Esther waiting to blossom!

Serving the poor helps my heart as much as it helps the person being served. Jesus said "the poor you will always have with you" (Matthew 26:11), and it may be that they will always be with us in order to help our hearts. My heart needs to learn the compassion and grace that serving the poor provides.

—Sally Hooper, Dallas, Texas

Jesus was never too busy to help those in need. He touched the untouchable and loved the unlovable. He served because he cared—not out of duty or guilt. It feeds my soul to help the poor.

—Chris Fuqua, Los Angeles, California

If we're not serving the poor, we are missing a part of Jesus' ministry. As leaders we must set the example for others in loving and serving those in need. It helps our hearts to love as Jesus did.

—Jan Jordan, Philadelphia, Pennsylvania

Sometimes we may ask "What can I do to help the poor?" Just like you, they also want attention, compassion, and respect. For attention, you need to give them some time and listen. For compassion, you need to put yourself in their shoes. For respect, you need to genuinely see them as the same person as you, which they are. If you do these things, you will not ask how to help. You will know.

—Joanne Webber, Los Angeles, California

PROFILE

Jenny Blenko, La Paz, Bolivia and New York, USA: Serving the Poor

by Jenny Blenko

Jenny Blenko is a courageous young woman who has focused her life on serving the poor.

A typical day at work: Today at work, I found out that one of the homeless boys we work with got drunk last night and killed another. I spent an hour listening to one of the women I work with share her story of abuse, and her thoughts of wondering if she will be able to financially support her two young daughters if she leaves her abuser. I then comforted that woman's friend as she told me that she sees her teenage son entering a pattern of alcoholism, and fears that he will one day be the abuser to another woman and their children. I ran into another one of the women I work with who told me that she found a dead baby in the trash last night as she was sweeping the streets.

Unfortunately, this journal entry reveals a normal day for me as I work with families who live and work on the streets of La Paz, Bolivia. I came to La Paz as a recent college graduate with degrees in social work and global health, expecting to see immense physical poverty. But when my plane touched down in this two-mile high city in the second poorest country in the hemisphere, I quickly saw that the poverty extends far beyond what initially meets the eye.

Shame, abuse, loneliness, insecurity, and distrust plague the lives of many of the beautiful families that I work with. The emotional and spiritual poverty that they face is overwhelming. Men line the streets to shoeshine in masks because they are too ashamed to be seen making their living in a way that is met with so much discrimination. Old women sit on corners prostituting themselves, because they believe that they have no other way to provide for their children and grandchildren. Eighty percent of the women I work with have suffered from physical and sexual abuse. Many children grow up alone because their parents need to work for twelve hours a day just to be able to put food in their mouths and a roof over their heads.

My job here is to help families save money to work their way out of poverty. However, I see my role as much more than coordinating services for them and making sure that they have goals and are saving. My job is to listen to the secrets they have fearfully hidden for years, to tell them and their children how beautiful and special and important they are, to kiss them and hug them and to make them laugh, to advocate for them when they feel as if no one else in the world is there, to spend weekends at their homes being a part of their lives, and to love them as much as possible in whatever crazy and imperfect way I can. My job is to be as much like Jesus as I possibly can. I know well that what they need is not me, but to *see God* through me. They need to see and know God, their all-powerful Maker and their Father who loves them more than life.

In John 3:30, the Bible says, "He must become greater; I must become less." In Psalm 31:16, David writes, "Let your face shine on your servant; save me in your unfailing love." As I venture into the streets every day, unsure what will come my way, these scriptures are the prayers that are written on my heart—that as I dance or pray or play or cry, people will not see me, but *God in me*. I pray that I can know his face so that mine can be a reflection of his. I pray that I can better understand his unfailing love so that I can better share his unfailing love. I pray that the families I work with can know my God—the God who has stooped down and rescued me, the God who carries me and calls me by name.

Soon I will leave La Paz and move to New York City to pursue my master's degree in international social work in a city that feels a world away. Even though I will be with students and social workers instead of children and *cholitas* (the Bolivian slang term for Andean indigenous women), I know that shame, abuse, loneliness, insecurity, and distrust will still surround me. The truth is that spiritual poverty is an epidemic that is not limited to any one country or culture. The people I will meet in New York City may live lives that are far removed from the lives of my families in La Paz, but they will still need to be told how special and important they are. They still need to be listened to without judgment and to be loved and made to laugh. Everyone needs Jesus just the same: New Yorkers, Bolivians, the rich, the poor, social workers, prostitutes, the happy, the sad—everyone.

We are each planted in different cities, countries, jobs, and situations, but we are all needed in this spiritual battle. As disciples, we all share the same blessing. We have the great gift of being able to show Jesus to those around us through our hearts, our faces, our words, our actions, our relationships, our lives. And we each share the same promise in Proverbs 11:25: "He who refreshes others will himself be refreshed." As it says in 2 Corinthians 9:15: "Thanks be to God for his indescribable gift!"

Leadership and Chemistry

CHAPTER NINETEEN

The Women of Romans 16: Leadership and Relationships

Jeanie Shaw

Romans 16

Memories stirred within the hearts of the women as they heard their names mentioned. Many of them had become Christians because of the Apostle Paul's teaching. Now he had sent a letter to the church in Rome, where they lived, to further teach and encourage the disciples there. They were eager to hear his words of encouragement.

Phoebe felt a sense of relief and encouragement as Paul's words were read. Tears welled up in Priscilla's eyes as she remembered Paul and the life-threatening situations they had endured together as they shared their faith. Mary remembered the long journeys alongside Paul while they cared for people's needs and shared the truth about Jesus. Rufus' mother smiled as she thought of the many times Paul had shared a meal with her and her son. She had always tried to prepare his favorite food. She relished those times, remembering their shared prayers, tears, and laughter around the dinner table.

As the women heard Paul's greetings they felt closer to God, closer to Paul, and closer to each other. They, through God's Spirit, had become connected through spiritual relationships. How had these relationships been built?

In Paul's greetings here in Romans 16 and also in Philemon, we can learn much from the types of relationships he had with women like Tryphosa, Persis, Apphia, and Phoebe. Paul describes them as fellow soldiers, fellow workers, and dear friends. They, like Paul, had great impact on the people whose lives they touched.

Note Paul's descriptions of his relationships with sisters in Romans 16:1–16:

- Phoebe served the church, and Paul held her in high regard. He described her as a fellow worker, soldier, and dear friend.

  I commend to you our sister Phoebe, a servant of the church in Cenchrea. I ask you to receive her in the Lord in a way worthy of the saints and to give her any help she may need from you, for she has been a great help to many people, including me. (v. 1)

- Priscilla, a fellow worker, risked her life for Paul; Mary was considered a fellow worker.

  Greet Priscilla and Aquila, my fellow workers in Christ Jesus. They risked their lives for me. Not only I but all the churches of the Gentiles are grateful to them. ...Greet Mary, who worked very hard for you. (vv. 3–4, 6)

- Paul considered Stachys his dear friend. Tryphena and Tryphosa were fellow hard workers.

  Greet Urbanus, our fellow worker in Christ, and my dear friend Stachys. ...Greet Tryphena and Tryphosa, those women who work hard in the Lord. (vv. 9, 12)

- Persis was a dear friend and fellow worker, and Rufus' mother had been a mother to Paul as well.

  Greet my dear friend Persis, another woman who has worked very hard in the Lord. Greet Rufus, chosen in the Lord, and his mother, who has been a mother to me, too. (vv. 12–13)

Then as now, we can have dear friends, fellow workers, and fellow soldiers come into our lives, forged on spiritual battlefields and in our shared labor for the Lord. These relationships are vital to our spiritual health and growth, and to our effectiveness as spiritual leaders. Spiritual leadership without these types of relationships is ineffective—as we reflect Jesus through our relationships (see John 13:34–35).

Fellow soldiers

In the big picture, as disciples we all are fellow soldiers—because we have the same King, battle, and enemy.

Endure hardship with us like a good soldier of Christ Jesus. No one serving as a soldier gets involved in civilian affairs—he wants to please his commanding officer. Similarly, if anyone competes as an athlete, he does not receive the victor's crown unless he competes according to the rules. (2 Timothy 2:3–5)

Jonathan said to his young armor-bearer, "Come, let's go over to the outpost of those uncircumcised fellows. Perhaps the LORD will act in our behalf. Nothing can hinder the LORD from saving, whether by many or by few." (1 Samuel 14:6)

It's vital to remember that we are in a battle. Sometimes we can get busy living life, even doing good works for God. I know at times I can forget that I'm in a battle. This happens when I rely on myself, desire to be comfortable, or forget that Satan is behind all sin and discord. I forget when I lack urgency in sharing my faith, don't want to do hard jobs, or think too much about things of this world. A spiritual leader is a fellow soldier because she remembers that she is in a battle against Satan. She needs the people around her to share in this battle, and others need her. I remember the battle when I am encouraged and convicted by the Scriptures, when fellow soldiers and I study the Bible with people who are not yet Christians, and when we work together to help sisters deepen their convictions and repent of sins. I remember I'm in a battle when we labor in prayer together and take risks together. I am inspired to go into battle by the courage of other sisters around me.

We need each other in the spiritual battle. We need help from each other with our own personal temptations and battles with Satan...fear, lack of self-discipline, anger, marriage issues, parenting problems, and so on, as well as the battle to save the lost and *keep* the saved saved. We need to be armor-bearers and we need armor-bearers.

Fellow workers

The women Paul mentioned in Romans 16 had different jobs, life situations, and fields of service, but they all had hard work in common. There is a lot of work in leadership. It takes work to consider needs of others. It takes work to apply the Scriptures to others' lives. It takes work to pray, to make phone calls, to encourage, and to go where God needs us. It takes work to have people into our homes and to practice hospitality. It takes work to follow up with others, to answer and initiate calls and e-mails. It takes work to visit the sick and help the poor. It takes work to equip others for the work of ministry. We can do all we can and we can work hard—but we can't do everything. We need God first and foremost, and then we need each other. We need each other to share the load and to gain encouragement and confidence from each other.

I believe Paul felt a closeness and kinship to the sisters he mentioned because they worked together for the glory of God. Think of relationships where you have worked hard together. It is bonding. You are able to use different strengths and talents. We are better together than by ourselves.

Dear friends

When the foundation of friendship between us as sisters is one of being fellow soldiers and fellow workers, friendship follows with greater ease. Jesus, by his example, shows us how to be friends. Consider Jesus' example of friendship in the following situations:

- Jesus noticed another's emotion. He was observant and caring. (Luke 7:11–15)
- Jesus showed that he cared. (John 20:15)
- Jesus shared in his friends' emotions, and wept with them. (John 11:33–35)
- Jesus did thoughtful things for his friends. (John 21:12)
- In the Garden of Gethsemane Jesus vulnerably expressed his pain and his need for his friends. (Mark 14:32–42)
- Jesus, the Son of God, was approachable. (Matthew 19:13–16)
- Jesus said he called the people close to him friends, because he held nothing back from them. (John 15:15)

Relationship busters

These descriptions of relationships are not the only possible results that come from working together. When we don't build spiritual relationships, we are often left disappointed and:

- *Burned out.* This happens when we are over-responsible in a relationship, thinking it all depends on us, instead of letting God work.
- *Lonely.* Relationships can be superficial rather than engaged if they are simply a relationship "in theory," without true involvement in each other's lives.
- *Isolated.* When we are independent versus interdependent, we project an attitude of "I don't need you; I'm all set." We cannot build effective relationships, and cannot work as a team with others.
- *Condescending.* If others around us are unhappy in their relationship with

us, it could be that we act as if we are over or under people, rather than functioning as fellow workers who treat each other with mutual respect.
- *Faking it.* When we withhold honest exchange from each other, we will lack true closeness.
- *Faithless.* If we settle for maintained weakness versus character growth (adopting an attitude of "that's just her," without expecting change), we can become faithless.
- *Frustrated.* We become frustrated or frustrating if we allow each other to remain ineffective, instead of helping each other to grow in effective ministry skills.
- *Compromised.* When we don't lead by example in our work and friendship, our leadership is compromised.
- *Stressed.* When relationships produce a burdensome chemistry instead of the joy and peace that come from the company of willing partners, they bring stress to our lives. Have you ever felt happy because someone was moving away, or felt a meeting was easier because someone wasn't there?
- *Stuck.* When there are inadequate and disunified convictions instead of convictions that build healthy ministry, we get stuck in our relationships. Do we share the same convictions about building ministry?
- *Discouraged.* When we are critical and negative, we end up discouraged, and we may discourage others.

- What does your life look like when you forget you're in a battle?
- What are practical ways that we, as fellow soldiers, can be armor-bearers who encourage others to go into spiritual battle? What are ways we can dream to advance the battle?
- How does hard work help our relationships? What happens in relationships where you don't work together for the Lord?
- What makes you feel friendship with others? (For example, I value attributes such as honesty, trust, listening, laughing, and vulnerability.) What are ways you can put into practice some of the ways Jesus expressed his friendship?

As we become more like the women of Romans 16—being fellow soldiers, fellow workers, and dear friends to one another—God will be glorified, and our relationships will be an eternal blessing.

God designed us for relationships! We need him—we need each other. Through these relationships we learn how to be loved and how to love. Some of the hardest relationships may be the very ones that are helping us to become more like Christ!

—Gloria Baird, Los Angeles, California

You can accomplish much during fellowship times if you practice Hebrews 10:24—and consider what others need. First seek out those visiting, then those struggling, then those in your ministry, then your closest friends. "Be there" in times of sickness, hurt, death, and pain. Showing up is more important than what you say.

—Jeanie Shaw, Burlington, Massachusetts

Relationships do not just happen. They have to be created, formed, molded, worked on, nurtured, evaluated and re-evaluated, revised, and valued. They cannot be ordered or forced, but they can be threatened and taken for granted. If we do not put into them as much as we take out, they can also be lost.

—Joanne Webber, Los Angeles, California

It's fascinating to see the interactions between Jesus and his disciples. They clearly regarded him as their rabbi, and yet he was so casual with them, so welcoming. He was never pompous or demeaning. He hung out with them as friend to friend. He invited them over to his place and visited their homes. He didn't pontificate; instead, he told them relatable stories. He performed amazing miracles in their presence, but never sought adulation or servitude. He never asked them to do anything that he had not demonstrated for them. Godly leadership is about relationship, or it is not leadership at all.

—Linda Brumley, San Diego, California

PROFILE

Cristina Lombardi, Milan, Italy: Relationships

by Cristina Lombardi

Cristina Lombardi's story is an inspiring demonstration of how God's tremendous love, grace, and power can reach across the world.

One September day, after coming back from my holidays in Turkey, I was feeling a void inside even though I had a "good life." I thought I would like to have someone near to me…a boyfriend. While I was in Turkey, a native of the village where I had spent my holidays told me about Facebook and gave me his name to find him should I need information about Turkish music, which had interested me. When I came back to work, my colleagues also told me about Facebook, and so being curious (like many women), I subscribed and looked for my Turkish friend. One of my colleagues started looking for people with his last name, and we started a competition for finding the most people with our last name. Since my last name was Lombardi, I started looking for all the Lombardis in the world. I sent many friendship requests, and among them I found Nick Lombardi, who was a seventeen-year-old guy from Philadelphia, and a disciple of Jesus.

Nick continually wrote on his wall about God. I was interested, because while I was in Turkey I had spoken with a Turkish man about his passion for Allah and the Qur'an. So, when I saw Nick writing on his Facebook wall with this love and passion about God, I sent him a message inquiring about the religion he professed. He accepted my request and wrote me about his faith and the things he believes.

A couple of days later we started "chatting" on Facebook. We talked about God, and I told him it was difficult for me to believe in God when something bad happened in life. Though I had once believed, I asked Nick why God permitted bad things to happen. I told about one of my best friends who had died suddenly the year before, leaving behind her husband and two young children. "Why," I asked Nick, "does God permit such things to happen?"

Nick was encouraging as we talked about pain and hard times and the way God allows pain to happen—but works for our good. He spoke with me about his faith and asked me if I used to go to a church. I told him I was Catholic, but that it had been a long time since I had gone to church. I also told him that my friend who passed away had invited me several times to a church she and her husband were part of, but I had always refused.

Near the end of our conversation, Nick asked me where I lived. Knowing that I was Italian, he had been hoping I lived in Milan, where there was a church in his fellowship. When I told him I lived in Milan, he said this could not be a coincidence. He gave me the Web site of the church in Milan and said goodbye.

After that conversation I called the husband of my friend who had died—his name was Giovanni—and asked him about the church. Amazingly, it was the same church! This was not a coincidence, but was the working of God. I spoke with Nick in another Facebook chat, and he told me that this was God still searching for me. Through my deceased friend, God was giving me another chance to listen to his call. She had invited me many, many times, and I had continually refused her. Now God was calling me again…through Facebook! I decided to go to the church. I called my friend Giovanni and told him I would like to go to church on Sunday. After that first time, I never missed.

The first time I visited was very difficult and sad for me. I was thinking of my friend, and I cried often. However, I decided to study the Bible, and a few months later I was baptized. It was so special and touching as my friend's husband and her daughter were there with me. I was so happy because I was going to become God's daughter, a member of God's family—and be forgiven from my sins.

Now I feel so happy and light. My only regret is that I could not share this moment with my friend, Elena, and that I didn't reply to God's call some years ago.

Note from Annie Silipo (women's ministry leader in Milan):

God had even more plans for Cristina's life. Cristina and Giovanni kept up their friendship. Over time, it grew and blossomed into a romantic interest. They are now married, and the entire family is doing well and continues to impact many others.

CHAPTER TWENTY

Lois and Eunice: Leadership and Training

Jeanie Shaw

2 Timothy 1:5

I have been reminded of your sincere faith, which first lived in your grandmother Lois and in your mother Eunice and, I am persuaded, now lives in you also. (2 Timothy 1:5)

Lois smiled as she watched her daughter, Eunice, repeat scriptures over and over again to Timothy. A young boy, Timothy would repeat the phrases his mother was teaching him. He looked to his mother and his grandmother for smiles of approval. Everywhere they went, Lois and Eunice would point out the beautiful creation that God had made. At night as they gazed at the stars, Lois told Timothy about the promise God fulfilled to Abraham, giving him more children than stars in the sky. Eunice piped in, explaining to Timothy that God knows the stars by name. As Timothy picked up rocks and threw them in to the river, his mom and grandmom told him the story of David's defeat of Goliath with stones and a slingshot. Over time, the stories, the scriptures, and the prayers took root deeply in young Timothy's heart. This foundational seed began to grow until Timothy was old enough to gain a faith of his own.

A lot of life is encompassed in 2 Timothy 1:5. This brief passage represents a grandmother's and a mother's years of prayers, godly living, and teaching young Timothy the Scriptures—and how to apply them to his thinking, speech, and interactions with others. This training would have required time, consistency, encouragement, correction, and example—all applied day after day, again and again. Perhaps Eunice did much of this training as a single mom, since Timothy's dad is not mentioned here. Or perhaps Timothy's father was present but an unbeliever (Acts 16:1 tells us that he was Greek) and did not offer spiritual training. Either way, Lois (Timothy's grandmother) and Eunice (his mother) were recognized for the legacy of faith they passed on to their grandson and son.

The source of our training

The root of the training given by Lois and Eunice was their sincere faith. In the same way for you and for me, our impact is rooted in the sincerity of our faith. Ultimately, integrity of faith won't and can't be hidden. Our actions always spring from that which is in our hearts. In the same way, religious practices can't substitute for or cover over shallow or nonexistent faith. Our children see through our hypocrisy. They will remember the way we live out our faith—sincerely or insincerely. The good news, however, is that no matter our age or stage of life, the genuine faith we live and teach is within our control. Even if we did not learn how to live a godly life while we were growing up, and now we are still learning how to do it, we can receive training from spiritual sisters who can help us.

I was extremely blessed to have had parents who loved God deeply, studied his word, continued to grow as they aged, and lived in a way that matched the convictions they held dear. Their example of putting God and his church as their first priority was always evident to me. Even when I tried to rebel from God and their training, I was drawn back by their example and the love and respect for God they had instilled in me.

It is important for mothers to realize that our spiritual leadership begins at home. Never underestimate the value of your influence on the "Eunices" and "Timothys" in your life—even as you pick up the toys for the umpteenth time, hold the vomit bucket, mediate a quarrel, or dry your child's tears. The spirituality you practice and the way you talk about your God will continue to have profound impact for years and generations to come. If your children have not yet made the decision to follow God, never quit praying, and never allow the "home fires" of unconditional love and Christlikeness to die in your own heart. Live with the faith, joy, and peace that you hope your children will grow to imitate one day. Your life will continue to have influence even when you don't see the result right away. And remember that you will also affect your "spiritual children" within the family of God.

My parents have both passed from this life. At both of their funerals, their lives were honored—and their love for God is the part of their lives that had the greatest impact. I wish to share the words of Sam Laing, who spoke about my dad at his funeral:

"He loved the Bible, but more so he loved the Author. And he loved people. The booming voice, the beaming smile, the bone-crushing hugs—what a beautiful, selfless soul he had! He would turn from any compliments and give full glory to God—and well he should—but dear, beloved brother these words are true, and to accept them is to recognize in your life the great work of the Holy Spirit—that Spirit of whom you so often spoke.

You cannot know of the immense influence you wielded on a generation of students—students who trusted and admired you. I was and am one of them. I always knew if you were in the picture, we would stay close to God and to his word.

Thank you. Thank you for giving your life freely, joyfully, tirelessly. Thank you for noticing the "smallest of these" and lifting them up. Thank you for every smile, every laugh, every greeting, every scripture, every hug, every tear of joy and humility that you shed so easily. Thank you for your forgiving heart that always believed the best in us all."

My mother was deaf during her last decades of life, and was a quieter soul. However, her influence was felt by many because of the way she loved her God. I am extremely grateful, and do not take lightly the scripture, "From everyone who has been given much, much will be demanded" (Luke 12:48). (Truthfully, by the grace of God we have all been given more than we could ever deserve, because we have been given the gift of God's Son.)

I share these things because this is the kind of legacy that I also pray to leave behind. I could wish for nothing more than a life that touches others because of the way I love God and live for him. How about you?

Spiritual leadership was likely not the goal of Lois and Eunice. It was the by-product of sincere faith expressed in wholehearted devotion to God. The training they passed on encourages me because it is simple in origin—stemming from sincere faith and constant use of the Scriptures.

Who needs training?

The truth is, we all need training in various areas. If we have grown up in dysfunctional families, we need to spend time learning about relationships from the Scriptures, and we need to spend time observing and imitating the spiritual habits of those who think and interact in godly ways. Whatever our background, we always have new things to gain from others. Spiritual leadership begins with the realization that we have not "arrived," and therefore we will always need to continue learning. Through this, we model a "learner's spirit." Eunice exhibited this quality, since she had obviously learned many godly qualities from her mother, Lois. We can't pass on a spirit of eagerness to learn and grow without modeling it ourselves.

In what ways do you seek to grow? Do you read, study, ask questions, and seek out opportunities to be further trained? Do you also seek out ways you can pass on the things you have learned to others? Sometimes we forget how much we have learned through our knowledge of the Scriptures, our life experiences, and from the godly examples we have seen. When we don't pass on the things we have learned, we stand in the way of God's plan. Paul encourages us, "Pass on what you heard from me—the whole congregation saying Amen!—to reliable leaders who are competent to teach others" (2 Timothy 2:2, MSG).

Perhaps Lois and Eunice trained many others, or perhaps they were timid. We don't know, but we do learn from the Scriptures that Timothy needed further training from Paul to grow beyond his timidity. When we let our timidity keep us from sharing the things we have learned, we limit God's plan for training. In Titus 2, older women are charged to train the younger women in spiritual matters—especially in marriage and parenting.

Essentials for training

While training often happens unintentionally—while we are not specifically focused on training—godly influence will have an even greater impact when we "train on purpose." This begins with the conviction that God calls us to present each other mature in Christ. When we realize how much we have been given, we will seek to give back. We must first model God's plan for living, and then look for ways to share this spiritual vision. We begin by sharing the biblical foundation for our convictions, and then help others (as we ourselves have learned) to apply these foundations and principles to all areas of life.

This process is most effective when we commit to each other a practical plan to make measurable progress. Training implies more than teaching. Training means that we consistently (with spaced repetition) model and apply biblical principles to the real-life situations in people's lives. We help other women learn how to study the Bible in context; we teach them to pray; we train them to be more effective in sharing the good news of Jesus; we train them to have meaningful conversations in fellowship; we train them to take their thoughts and minds captive, we teach them to cook; we teach them how to organize their homes; we teach them how to take care of their health; we teach them how to be respectful to their husbands; we teach them how to resolve conflicts; we train them to love and discipline their children—and the list goes on and on.

Training like this is a gift we give to each other, to help one another glorify God in the best way we can. What a blessing that God has given us friends, sisters, mothers, and grandmothers within his family—women to help equip us not just for a happy daily life, but for a spiritual life of fulfillment and usefulness.

> Instead, speaking the truth in love, we will in all things grow up into him who is the Head, that is, Christ. From him, the whole body, joined and held together by every supporting ligament, grows and builds itself up in love, as each part does its work. (Ephesians 4:15–16)

- What would you most want to be shared about you when your life is over?
- What are specific ways you show eagerness to learn and grow?
- In what areas of spiritual life do you feel most competent to train others?
- What holds you back from getting further training?
- What holds you back from training others?

Lois and Eunice trained out of their spiritual integrity. From Timothy's infancy, they taught him the things that made him "wise for salvation through faith in Christ Jesus." His life and teachings have impacted multitudes of people, including you and me. When we are trained, and then we train others out of our spiritual integrity, we may never know the extent to which we affect other's souls for eternity. But in the spirit of these women who came before us, let us learn all we can and give all we can, as God would have us do.

One of the most exciting things about life is that there is always more to learn! As we keep learning, then we can in turn teach what we have learned. In that way, training is ongoing and never-ending!
—Gloria Baird, Los Angeles, California

Help train parents to teach their children to love the kingdom of God above all.
—Roberta Balsam, Chicago, Illinois

We always need training . . . and to hear the Scriptures applied to our lives even when we know what we would tell others. Always use the Bible in your counseling, conversations, teaching, and discipling. Whether teaching two or two thousand, prepare well and inspire faith through the Scriptures.
—Jeanie Shaw, Burlington, Massachusetts

As women we get discouraged when we feel like someone should have picked up on the hints we have given or when we believe they should have initiated in a certain area. We need to stop and ask ourselves, "Have I ever taught her this, or that?" Jesus is the perfect example of teaching us little by little—with great patience and careful instruction. This requires a grace-filled ministry.
—Kim Evans, Philadelphia, Pennsylvania

PROFILE

Sarah Armstrong, Florida: Training

by Barbara Porter, Florida

It is so faith-building when God is able to produce an incredible victory out of what, without him, would be destined for defeat. Almost two years ago, Sarah Armstrong, a disciple in the South Florida Church of Christ, experienced the tragic breakup of her marriage when her husband of six years left her. Naturally, Sarah was deeply saddened by this sudden turn of events, as were her close friends. Sarah and her husband were soon divorced.

Just a few months later, the South Florida Church of Christ initiated its School of Missions, in which in-depth Bible studies are taught to disciples who desire either to grow in leadership or to become missionaries in South America. For several hours each Saturday morning, on her own initiative, Sarah faithfully attended the classes.

Sarah asked to talk to me one day after class. She expressed that before she had become a disciple and married, she had studied Spanish and had hoped someday to live in a Spanish-speaking country. She shared that she had considered and prayed a lot, and believed she was ready to make plans to move to South America. She looked at me and said something like, "After all, why should I sit around and mope as though my life were over?" All I could think was, *Wow! What faith!*

Soon after our conversation, the pieces began to fall into place and the doors began to open. A faithful and adventurous family—Francisco and Liz Bedoya and their two small children—had just arrived in Florida. Having neither a job nor much money, the Bedoyas had come to attend the School of Missions in the hopes of being able to fulfill their dream to lead a church in South America. Like Abraham and Sarah, they did not know where they would end up, but they were open to God's leading. Through the School of Missions, God connected the Bedoyas and the newly single Sarah, who all wanted to live out their dreams but did not yet know each other. Sarah worked on getting her certificate to teach English as a second language, while the Bedoyas simply prayed and waited.

You have probably already guessed the end of the story. Within less than six months, the Bedoyas had met, grown to love, and been hired by the church in Asunción, Paraguay, a church which had been without a leader for about six years! And just a few weeks later, Sarah left for Asunción, too—to work as an English teacher in the school where the Bedoyas' children are enrolled (they just happened to need an English teacher).

It takes a lot of courage to leave your job, home, family, and country to serve God and reach out to people of another culture and language. It takes even more courage to do so after you have just experienced a life-changing and heartbreaking event. But Sarah sees it differently: "I just want my brothers and sisters to know that there is no dream, no prayer, beyond God's reach for anyone—at any time, in any situation, anywhere."

Sarah spent three years in Paraguay, where she fell in love with the mission field and with the church in Asunción. While she taught English as a second language, she helped to lead one of her students to Christ. He is an amazing young man who has already served as a campus intern and is currently applying to the best universities in South America. Sarah is now back in the States, continuing to be used by God in her home country as she leads a group of single women.

CHAPTER TWENTY-ONE

Ruth and Naomi: Leadership and Mentoring

Robin Williams

The Book of Ruth

The famine was severe: fields barren, animals dying, children starving. In desperation, Naomi and her family—her husband and two sons—left Bethlehem and moved to Moab, where they hoped to find food to survive. But while they were living as foreigners in Moab, Naomi's husband died, her two sons married Moabite women, and then ten years later, her sons died.

After her son's deaths, Naomi's daughters-in-law clung to her. But all Naomi could think to do and say was, "Go home! I have nothing more to give you! I'm old; I can't produce any more sons for you, and even if I could, you'd be too old to marry them by the time they were ready. You're young; go home to your mother and let her help you find another man and live your life. How many times do I need to tell you? Go back to your home!" Three times Naomi told them to go home. After the second time, Ruth's sister-in-law, Orpah, returned to her mother's home. But Ruth would not be dissuaded. Ruth was determined to stay with Naomi, and stay she did.

As we read on in the book of Ruth, we see a beautiful relationship unfold. Naomi takes Ruth in as her daughter and teaches her about the God of Israel, and about building a life in her country—she even helps Ruth to find a husband! Their relationship is a wonderful example of a successful mentoring relationship, embodying the key qualities of respect, loyalty, diligence, and kindness. Throughout our lives, we will all need to play the role of mentor and mentee, several times over. And if we aspire to some form of spiritual leadership, mentoring will play a special role in our life—both as we learn to lead, and as we pass on our knowledge to others.

What can we glean about mentoring from Ruth and Naomi?

Respect and loyalty

What made Ruth want to stay with her mother-in-law? The world tells us in subtle and not-so-subtle ways that it is impossible to have a positive relationship with a mother-in-law. So why would Ruth give up her own family to be with Naomi? We could speculate many things, but one thing is for sure: Ruth respected Naomi.

Mentoring begins with respect. Ruth respected the life Naomi lived. For her to say, "Your people will be my people and your God my God" (1:16) means that she saw something in Naomi's life that she wanted. For ten years Ruth saw Naomi live without a husband. Perhaps she saw Naomi fight to find peace and acceptance as she learned to live her life alone. Maybe Naomi's dependence on God stood out to Ruth. Maybe Ruth saw that with God, Naomi could withstand and endure the pain of losing a husband—the pain Ruth herself now faced—even though at times Naomi felt mystified and depressed. Perhaps Ruth saw a strength in Naomi, the faith that believed God would be there to take care of her. Naomi must have been a deeply loving woman to inspire such affection and devotion from her daughters-in-law. Even through her grief, she gave selflessly to Ruth and Orphah and the rest of her family. I'm sure Ruth had many questions about Naomi's God, and Naomi patiently and lovingly shared all her knowledge and experiences with her. As Ruth heard these stories, she too came to believe, and she made Naomi's God her God.

This is what mentoring is all about: passing on to others what God has done for us. Jesus instilled this teaching in his disciples. As he said in Mark 5:19, "Go home to your family and tell them how much the Lord has done for you, and how he has had mercy on you." When we respect Jesus and understand people's need to know him, we will share with great patience and selflessness all that he has done for us. Naomi helped Ruth learn how to live God's way in their day.

We all need a spiritual woman in our life to teach us how to live for God. For some of us, that woman is our mother. I feel so blessed to have had a mother who passed on to me her devotion to God and her desire to live for him. She taught me through her self-denial, hard work, faith, perseverance, and love for God and people. For you, that woman may be an older sister (either biological or spiritual), a stepmother, a relative, or a friend. Even if our biological family lacked godliness, God can provide other women in our lives to help us learn how he wants us to live. This is the promise Jesus gives us in Mark 10:29–30:

> "I tell you the truth," Jesus replied, "no one who has left home or brothers or sisters or mother or father or children or fields for me and the gospel will fail to receive a hundred times as much in this

present age (homes, brothers, sisters, mothers, children and fields—and with them, persecutions) and in the age to come, eternal life."

Mentorship is not the only way God teaches us, but it is a means to helping us find our way more quickly. Mentors not only teach us the ways of God, they also show us the ways of God by how they live. We all need living examples of godly womanhood.

But not only did Ruth respect Naomi, Naomi also respected Ruth. From all accounts, Naomi was a strong-willed woman. At first she insisted it would be best for Ruth to go home to her own family—maybe Naomi felt too tired to continue caring and teaching and training young women; perhaps she was still overcome with grief; maybe she felt she was too old and had nothing left to give—but Ruth changed Naomi's mind. When Naomi heard her daughter-in-law's opinions and desires, she accepted them. She put Ruth's wishes and needs above her own.

If we are going to mentor someone, we need to respect them. We need to value what they think, feel, and want. When we value others, we become more than a teacher; we become a mentor who cares about the outcome of another's life. Naomi did as Paul says in Philippians 2:3: "Do nothing out of selfish ambition or vain conceit, but in humility consider others better than yourselves. Each of you should look not only to your own interests, but also to the interests of others."

In every good mentoring relationship, there is mutual respect. Mutual respect produces sincere affection and the kind of loyalty that lasts a lifetime.

Diligence and kindness

Can you imagine having to create a new life after famine and death have decimated your family? Naomi's situation was certainly one of the more difficult ones anyone could have to overcome. As she herself said, she was a bitter woman, and she renamed herself Mara (which means "bitter"). As we age, life can beat us up and make us feel like we have nothing to offer anyone. But even when we've been through heartbreak, God gives us opportunities, as he did with Naomi, to help other women benefit from our experiences. As we see with Naomi, even bitterness and hardships couldn't keep her from doing what she knew was right. Her relationship with God kept her going and overcoming severe obstacles. Whenever we have someone depending on us, as Ruth depended on Naomi, we find a way to do the right thing. Naomi knew that as a mother figure it was her responsibility to help Ruth find another husband. Mothers played a great role in finding husbands for their daughters in those times—not unlike mothers today. We may not directly arrange marriages for our daughters today (although some of us would like to!), but we do prepare them for life with their husbands. In the same way, when mature women mentor younger women in God's church, we can teach them how to look for a godly man and how to build a relationship that pleases God. And as we help others, we ourselves are changed. That's why we remember Naomi as *Naomi* (which means "pleasant") and not *Mara*; as she took care of Ruth, she became pleasant and happy again.

Naomi guided Ruth to be diligent and kind. Ruth took the initiative to work in the fields, looking for someone's favor. After she found the favor of Boaz, Naomi taught her to be even more industrious and generous. She gave her specific advice and encouraged her to give her all. Diligence and kindness stand out. Boaz viewed Ruth's actions as kindness (Ruth 3:10). Still today, women need to be taught and shown how to work hard and be generous with their love.

As Ruth followed Naomi's advice, she found a husband, but that is not the only purpose these qualities can achieve. Learning how to be diligent and kind enables us to do well in school, find good jobs, have great friendships. Good mentoring relationships help us find a plan for our lives and carry it out in a way that brings us fulfillment and peace.

Blessings and benefits

Ruth listened to Naomi's wise counsel, and her life was blessed. She married Boaz and had a child. She became the great grandmother of David, and ended up in the lineage of Jesus. Naomi's life was also blessed: she became a grandmother and rejoiced in caring for her grandson.

No matter where we are in life, we should always remain open to giving mentoring *and* receiving it. There are always things to learn and things to give; people who can teach us, and people who need our teaching. Sometimes we try to force all mentoring relationships into a single mold, but there are many different kinds of mentoring relationships, and they need not be limited by age. Anyone can be a mentor or a mentee on some level. Although it's great when our mentors are mature women with lots of life experience under their belts (like Naomi), older women are not the only ones qualified to mentor others. Age has certain advantages, but sometimes we can be mentored by someone who simply has more experience in a certain area than we do. What matters is how we are in the relationship. Ruth and Naomi show us the outcome of successful mentoring, and exemplify some of the qualities that make such relationships work.

Ruth and Naomi made each other better. Naomi taught Ruth to love God, and helped her build a marriage and family with a godly man. Ruth brought love and joy and hope back into Naomi's life when it seemed all hope was lost. They helped one another to rise above their grief and loss, and together they built a new family that had a lasting legacy—a legacy that stretched all the way to Jesus, and touches us even today.

- Do you have a mentor? What qualities are you hoping to learn from your mentor?
- If you don't have a mentor, do you want to find one? Is there anyone you admire who you would like to learn from?
- Are you mentoring anyone? If so, what are you trying to teach them? And if not, what are some ways you could see yourself helping or mentoring someone else?
- What would you most like to leave as your legacy?

As you enter into mentoring relationships, ask yourself these questions:
- Do you respect others as much as you want to be respected?
- Is loyalty based on mutual respect?
- Is diligence a part of your work ethic?
- Is generosity at the heart of everything you do?
- Do you follow advice wholeheartedly?
- Do you give advice lovingly?

God brings people into our lives for a reason. Take a look at the women around you, and take advantage of opportunities to learn and to give. Embrace the people God has given you with respect, loyalty, diligence, and kindness. Relationships are a precious gift from him. Don't waste them—let God use those relationships to bless you, to shape you, and to fully use you for his purposes.

Talk with those you are training as you plan lessons, in order to impart the way you think. We want to teach the heart as much as anything—so they can learn to think in their own situations.

— Geri Laing, Lake Worth, Florida

In order for people to listen to what we have to say, they generally need to feel that we care and that we can relate to their situation.

Mary Lou Craig, Boonton, New Jersey

No matter our age, we all need to be learners and teachers—mentors and mentees. While we learn through all kinds of situations and through many people, our growth becomes more deliberate and effective when it is clear to both people that we are intentionally mentoring and/or being mentored.

—Jeanie Shaw, Burlington, Massachusetts

One of the greatest ways we can mentor others is by modeling repentance. Everybody needs a good picture of what humble repentance looks like.

—Virginia Lefler, Chicago, Illinois

Leadership development requires investment on the part of the people doing the training. This includes regular times spent together—praying, developing character, learning people skills, and serving others. Leadership by example is important.

—Helen Nanjundan, London, United Kingdom

PROFILE

Diddy Tempo Akello, Burundi: Mentoring

by Diddy Tempo Akello

It is often difficult to understand life beyond our familiar borders. Many Christian women face challenges so different from ours. Diddy Tempo Akello, who lives in Central Africa, helps women who have grown up in the chaos and heartbreak of tribal war to come to know the God of forgiveness. As we see the lives of women such as Diddy, we can be inspired to push through the challenges we face—and never quit. The time she spends mentoring women makes a profound difference in their lives. Diddy shares with us a peek into her life as a disciple in Central Africa:

Have you ever walked in a dangerous place and felt that there were many land mines, but you hoped and believed that the next ten miles would be better? This is how I feel about my beautiful country, Burundi. It is a small country in Central Africa nicknamed "the heart of Africa," or "the country of a thousand and one mountains."

While growing up, I was amazed at the love of Burundians. People would walk many miles without knowing where their next meal would come from or where they would sleep. When they tired from their journey, they would often knock on my door—and there they would find all they needed. My parents taught me to treat people like I would like to be treated myself. It was not until later in life that I learned this is a biblical truth (Matthew 7:12).

Shortly before I became a disciple, a civil war broke out in my country. Love was replaced by hatred in the hearts of many. We began to look at each other differently—according to the physical features of the three existing ethnic groups. People began killing each other in their own neighborhoods—even their own closest family members. A husband would kill another man's wife and children if they were from different ethnic groups. It was during this time that God reached out to me and I became a disciple. As a young Christian, I had the dream of evangelizing my city, Bujumbura, the capital of Burundi.

Everyone was hurting around me, and many are still suffering to this day. Ten years of guerilla war left poverty and insecurity.

In order to see my dream become a reality, I decided to pray about everything. I do not want to let the circumstances around me stop me from helping my town find God. Every day I meet women who ask me why a good God would allow her enemies to kill all of her family members—sometimes even in their presence. They ask me why he let the rebels rape them. We cry together as they recall these traumatic moments. I continually share God's love and God's plan and his desire to see evil destroyed. I speak of God's forgiveness that not only shows us how to forgive, but also empowers us to offer forgiveness. I believe I live in Bujumbura and not in Kenya, my husband's country, for this very reason. I have seen God work through me to help the women here come to love God deeply.

I wish I could say those are the only challenges I face, but I (and my family) also face health challenges. These bring me to my knees. Since I was young, I have suffered from migraines and also a recurrent sleep disorder. My husband fights chronic migraines and recently was diagnosed with high blood pressure. Our three children also have chronic health problems. Hospital visits are a regular part of our lives. In the middle of these challenges, God has been faithfully taking care of the sisters' ministry and adding to our number. Each hour or two in the ministry makes a big difference in my life, and in the lives of the beautiful ladies in this town. This is the way we can affect our whole country. I make it my goal to get together with each of the thirty sisters at least once a month. I desire to be a great and inspiring friend to all. This is possible because the city is very small—it is a village, not because it is small and rugged, but because everybody knows everybody. I am excited to help many women find the beautiful life Jesus promised, where there will be no tears—and yes, I know that the next ten miles will be better because they are walked with Jesus, who loves, strengthens, and forgives us.

CHAPTER TWENTY-TWO

Euodia and Syntyche: Leadership and Conflict

Jeanie Shaw

Philippians 4:2-3

Tension filled the room. Euodia and Syntyche were at it again. It seemed that every time one of them had a suggestion, the other one had a better idea. Everyone noticed the way they looked away from each other instead of toward each other. Their body language conveyed a relationship that had grown as cold as ice. It seemed that the two women were in competition with each other—wanting to be heard more than they wanted to understand. The atmosphere in the room with them was unpleasant, as their disunity was obvious. Before long, everyone else's conversations began revolving around the women and their division. Some people began to take sides. Others wondered if they even remembered how their conflict had started. Though the conflict was obvious—like the proverbial elephant in the living room—for some reason people gingerly walked around the elephant as if it wasn't there. No one seemed to have enough courage, or perhaps enough love, to help them come to resolution.

One thing was certain. Euodia and Syntyche were women of impact… so much so that the Apostle Paul focused attention on them in his letter to the Philippian church—pleading with them to get resolved, and calling on others to help them in this resolution. They were women of such influence that we still read about their conflict today.

How would you like your claim to fame to be that of disunity? If you carry unresolved issues in your heart it could be. Never underestimate the impact of your life—for good or for bad—and don't underestimate the far-reaching influence of unresolved conflict. We may think our "personal" issues don't affect anyone else, but these women gained the attention of their entire church. They got the attention of the whole world.

Spiritual leaders resolve conflict.

Spiritual leaders resolve their own conflicts, and spiritual leaders also help others to resolve their conflicts. Too often we avoid difficult conversations—or conflicts of any kind. When that happens, we can become "people-pleasers" and stuff the things we really feel inside. Sometimes after a time of "stuffing," one action or word can result in an explosion of our pent-up emotions and hurtful words. Others of us may try to ignore our ill feelings toward someone, hoping that the feelings (or the person) will just go away. This method never works. Unresolved feelings of disunity fester and grow.

Others of us may be among those who "run to the fight." Perhaps we grew up in a family where voices were raised and tempers flared. We have not become accustomed to the "calm and gentle spirit" the Bible instructs us to have as part of our character (1 Peter 3:4). When we think we are having a "normal conversation," another person may hear anger in the tone of our voice. We will never resolve conflict until we learn to obey the Scriptures and "be completely humble and gentle" (Ephesians 4:2). It is a wise practice to read scriptures (such as this one) before resolving a conflict in order to remember God's instructions for us. During their quarrel, Euodia and Syntyche detracted from God's church instead of building it up.

Settle matters quickly.

The Scriptures tell us not to let the sun go down on our anger, which gives the devil a foothold (Ephesians 4:26–27). We may be able to think of situations where conflict with others has lingered for days, weeks, and even years. This is not God's plan. He calls on us to settle matters quickly. He tells us that if we have something against someone or know someone has something against us, resolution takes precedence even over "offering our gift at the altar" (Matthew 5:23–24). Energy that could and should be used to help people in need is sacrificed when we let quarrels and disunity linger. Disunity creates tension and fatigue among those involved and the people whose lives they touch. Stress and tension takes the place of peace and unity.

Spiritual leaders must be counted on to have a calm and gentle demeanor. If people around you feel they need to "walk on eggshells," or if they pray you are in a good mood when needing to discuss something, then the "spiritual" part of your leadership needs work—and repentance.

Finding resolution

Often we *sort* of address disunity—that is, we talk around it and about it, without being honest and forthright. The Bible calls us to speak the truth in love to one another. The Scriptures also call us to go to the person we have something against in order to resolve the situation. If we can't resolve it, then we are to bring someone in to help us (Matthew 18:15–17). It is most helpful for those involved to mutually agree on one or two mature and spiritual brothers and/or sisters in Christ to help them resolve a conflict when they cannot do it by themselves. Euodia and Syntyche did not do this. They were at fault—as were their brothers and sisters for not helping them. Paul had to call for reinforcement. In Matthew 18, Jesus says that if the people brought into the situation can't help us find unity, then the issue is to be brought before the whole church! Most people are able to find resolution before such a big step is taken. Would we really want the whole church to know about our disputes?

Further on in Matthew 18, Jesus teaches us the importance of forgiveness and grace in our relationships. We should begin the steps toward resolution by deciding to take personal responsibility whenever we can, and deciding to hear what the other person is saying. Rarely is a dispute completely one-sided. Forgiveness needs to be spoken and accepted. Words such as "I'm sorry," "please forgive me," and "I forgive you" are crucial in bringing about complete resolution. Often they are hard to say because it is difficult to be "completely humble and gentle" (Ephesians 4:2). However, this is the posture God calls for. Only at the foot of the cross can we find the humility to be wrong *and* the humility to be right.

When we help others find resolution, it is essential we approach the situation without bias. Proverbs 18:17 is crucial: "The first to present his case seems right, till another comes forward and questions him." It is also important to pray for wisdom. God promises that he will give wisdom to those who ask, "without finding fault" (James 1:5).

We also need to learn to accept each other when we have differences of opinion when there is no biblical or spiritual mandate given. We often won't think alike, but we need to learn to think together. It is never worth damaging a relationship in order to be "right" in your opinions. Often, "personality conflicts" are excuses for a lack of complete forgiveness and acceptance of one another.

The ability to resolve conflict is crucial for leaders. If leaders can't resolve their own conflicts, how will they be able help others? We may not always know how a conflict began, but we can always decide to take personal responsibility for our part, to be completely humble and gentle, to forgive, and to speak the truth in love. Leaders must learn to be honest—wisely, humbly and lovingly speaking up when they disagree, feel hurt, or think something is not righteous. Jesus prayed long and hard at the end of his time on earth for unity (John 17). Unity cannot be assumed or forced, but it must be forged.

The conflict between Euodia and Syntyche affected many people—not for the good. They needed help in order to make progress. Their unity was important to Paul, and important for the entire church. Paul pleaded with them to agree in the Lord. While they are never mentioned again, we assume the church helped them to come to complete unity. We know they were important women to Paul and had done a great deal of good for many. He referred to these sisters as his fellow workers—along with Clement and his other "fellow workers whose names are in the book of life" (Philippians 4:3). It is important to note that Paul did not give up on these sisters. These relationships were valuable to Paul and their church. The sisters were stuck and they needed help. Paul did not impugn their motives or discount their value as fellow disciples. Their unity mattered to him. He loved them enough to plead for their agreement and reconciliation. Will we love others in this way?

Do you allow conflict to keep going on between you and someone else? If so, how will you proceed in order to get this relationship "unstuck?"

- What are areas that often tempt you to get into conflict with someone?
- If you are involved in a conflict right now, what would resolution look like in the relationship? Do you value the relationship (and righteousness) enough to fight for it?
- What might hinder your ability to help others who are in a conflict?

What are important scriptures that apply to:
- The timeliness of resolving conflict?
- The attitudes we need to resolve conflict?
- The steps to take in order to resolve conflict?
- The importance of forgiveness in conflict?
- The importance of listening in order to resolve conflict?

Write these scriptures on your heart, and read them whenever you get "stuck" or need to help others get "unstuck."

Paul pleaded with Euodia and Syntyche to agree because unity in the church matters. Unity was all-important to Jesus, and it should be all-important to us. It's encouraging to remember that even Jesus' own disciples were not without conflict—and yet he always helped them to find resolution. Let's set the example of quickly resolving conflict in our own lives, and quickly helping others to restore unity in their relationships.

Having and giving respect for each other is key when you are in the midst of conflict—yet respect is often hard to give. It is vital to listen first, instead of reacting and assuming. It often helps to see conflict as something to be managed rather than a problem to be solved.
—Gloria Baird, Los Angeles, California

A very helpful perspective before conflict resolution is, "I could be wrong!"
—Mary Lou Craig, Boonton, New Jersey

Prayer with the others involved in the conflict plays a major part. Forgiveness/resolution comes a lot quicker if God is part of the conversation!
—Sally Hooper, Dallas, Texas

Leaders are often involved in helping disciples resolve their relationships. We need biblical wisdom when resolving conflict. Proverbs 18:17 comes into mind here. We cannot dispute God's word when it comes to preserving unity. We must call sin sin and not show partiality.
—Caron Vassallo, Melbourne, Australia

Remember that people can and will let you down and sin against you. Always keep your eyes fixed on Jesus, who will never let you down. We are all sinners and need our savior. He will help you see things in the right perspective so you won't become bitter and lose heart.
—Laura Fix, Londonderry, New Hampshire

PROFILE

Jean Dziedzinkski, Massachusetts: Conflict

by Jean Dziedzinski

Conflicts arise in all relationships, especially within marriages. Jean Dziedzinki's story of forgiveness overcoming conflict has inspired many others to have hope. She shares her story:

Frank and I married in 1991. We had both been married before and had children from those marriages. We are a blended family. Our blended family was less like a stirred pitcher of lemonade and more like the whirling of a blender on the "crush ice" setting. Our children were young and were dealing with the effects of life with divorced parents—and life was busy! We were naive about the difficulties blended families face and the stress it would place on our marriage. Cracks soon began to appear in our new "perfect" relationship.

When I became a disciple in 1994, I added various church activities to an already packed schedule—plus I started attending night school. Shortly after that time, I was laid off for the second time within two years. The woman Frank had married started to change, and he wasn't really sure what was going on. While I'd like to say that I became perfect after I was baptized, unfortunately I was still human, and although I was now saved, I still had my old sinful nature.

This stress, together with our sinful reactions, led to our separation in 1998. Our hopes for a wonderful new life together were fading fast. I was devastated. How could this be happening to me again? As I contemplated how to deal with our separation and possible divorce, God led me to a couple of key decisions:

First, I read all the scriptures on marriage and divorce. Jesus said in Matthew 19:8, "Moses permitted you to divorce your wives because your hearts were hard. But it was not this way from the beginning." I knew I didn't want a hard heart towards Frank and that I would have to fight to keep it soft. I decided that I would not seek a divorce—no matter what. I loved Frank and held out hope that we would reconcile.

My second decision was to be as personally righteous as possible—to the best of my ability with Jesus beside me—no matter what Frank did or said.

God reminded me that I would stand before him someday and give an account for my actions (Romans 14:12). As Matthew 6:14–15 says: "For if you forgive men when they sin against you, your heavenly Father will also forgive you. But if you do not forgive men their sins, your Father will not forgive your sins." My salvation depended on my ability to forgive.

We were separated for eight years as we tried various ways to resolve our issues. We went through some very painful times during these years. The battle to keep my heart soft was difficult, and often I would daily—or even hourly—beg God to help me forgive, trying to pull out any bitter sprout before it had a chance to root. Prayer, along with the support of my sisters in the kingdom, comforted and helped me. Remembering Jesus on the cross helped me to have enough perspective to keep going. I clung to God for dear life. The pain I suffered was nothing compared to dying a horrible painful death on a cross, bearing the sins of the world after having lived a sinless life. Jesus' words in Luke 23:34, "Father forgive them, for they do not know what they are doing," helped me remember that Frank was lost—he desperately needed God, and didn't know what he was doing. I could show him God's love and heart through my words and actions.

During this time I learned that God was faithful and trustworthy; I learned that I am not alone; I learned the power of prayer and how through prayer God can heal and comfort you in inexplicable ways; I learned that through the Spirit I can endure much more than I thought—past my own ability or patience. I learned that "I can do everything through him who gives me strength" (Philippians 4:13).

In 2007, after eight years of separation, we agreed to divorce. Heartbroken, we went to court. As a Christian, I had believed we were not beyond reconciliation, but I had always known it would be possible only with God. Now it seemed like there was no hope.

But as we walked out of the courthouse, I had no idea how God was working on Frank's heart. Over the next couple of years, God moved powerfully in Frank's heart. He wanted to know more about my faith, began studying the Bible, and was baptized.

On September 4, 2010, through our commitment to God and each other, we were remarried. No matter how much conflict you have experienced, God is a God of forgiveness and second chances. We are now able, as a couple united in Christ, to share the love we experience with others.

Every time I think about how God has healed our marriage and put our family back together, I think, "What is impossible with men is possible with God" (Luke 18:27). Praise God for his power to bring healing to even the most hopeless of situations.

CHAPTER TWENTY-THREE

Hagar: Leadership Overcomes Dysfunction
Jeanie Shaw

Genesis 16 and 21

Sex, slavery, pride, jealousy, abuse, prejudice, bullying, eviction and strife—these are ingredients for a television soap opera.

Hagar lived in a "soap opera" world. A maidservant to Sarai, she was commanded by her mistress to sleep with her mistress' husband. Thinking God couldn't follow through on his promise of a child, Sarai took matters into her own hands and planned a solution to her barrenness. And so began episode one.

Having conceived the "awaited child" for Abram and Sarai, Hagar was delighted—and had no problem letting her mistress know that she was now "one up" on her. She despised Sarai. She had the child, but Sarai had the love of the child's father. Sarai responded to Hagar with rage and jealousy—and she felt justified in mistreating her servant. Hagar fled for safety, as Sarai's abuse was too much for her to take. It was painful. Hagar felt she had no need for Sarai anyway. She had Abram's child. She was being treated unfairly and would stand for no more, so she left.

God was watching Hagar, and through an angel, he asked her where she had come from and where she was going. Hagar didn't know where she was going. She only knew she was running away. God told her to go back to Sarai. He told her to go back and put up with Sarai's abuse—unfair as it was. At first this seemed preposterous to Hagar. But God had spoken. He had called her by name. To Abram and Sarai, she was just a servant—but to God, she was Hagar. He assured her that he was watching her—he knew her misery, and her story was not over. He told her she was going to have a son, and promised her (just as he had promised Abram and Sarai) that her descendants would be too numerous to count.

An angel of GOD found her beside a spring in the desert; it was the spring on the road to Shur. He said, "Hagar, maid of Sarai, what are you doing here?"

She said, "I'm running away from Sarai my mistress."

The angel of GOD said, "Go back to your mistress. Put up with her abuse." He continued, "I'm going to give you a big family, children past counting."
(Genesis 16:7–10, MSG)

Going back to Sarai would surely be humiliating. It would be as if Sarai had "won." Yet Hagar went back.

God searches for us in dysfunction.

When people around you disregard God's plans and take matters into their own hands, it often affects the people all around them—including you. God was still with Hagar, even in the dysfunction that surrounded her. He didn't promise that her problems would go away. But God saw Hagar's misery, and he cared about her. He cares for you and me as well. He still has promises for us, even if we must encounter situations that aren't fair. God does not promise "fairness." He does promise he will be with us through difficulties, when we look to him.

Hagar found God through her misery.

What enabled Hagar to go back to live in a dysfunctional environment? She came to believe that God was with her and cared for her, even when life was not "fair." He became personal to her. She gave God a name: El-Roi, "the One who sees me" (Genesis 16:13).

Hagar believed that God saw her—and as a result, she was able to see God. When we believe, like Hagar, that God really sees us—that he knows us by name, cares about our feelings, and loves us deeply—then we can begin to see him for who he really is. When we see God involved in our life, it changes our perspective on everything.

Hagar's son, Ishmael, was born, and then later Sarah bore her promised son, Isaac. As Ishmael grew, his character revealed more about Hagar's complicated relationship with Sarah. Our children find the strengths in our character, but they also find the cracks. When Hagar was pregnant, she had become prideful and taunted Sarah. It is therefore no surprise that Ishmael, in a similar way, bullied Isaac—even though Isaac was much younger. Perhaps Ishmael and Hagar, feeling insecure, second-rate, and unloved, were trying too hard to prove their worth. If they had only relied on the love and value God gave them, perhaps they would not have felt the need to put Sarah and Isaac down through mocking.

Sarah responded badly. She took charge and gave her husband an ultimatum, insisting that he throw "that slave woman" and "that slave woman's son" out of the house (Genesis 21:10). She did not care where they went—to her they were just nameless properties competing for Abraham's attention and love, and for her son's inheritance. She would have none of that. This was not Sarah's finest hour; however, God is a God of redemption, and both of these women found their way back to God. Abraham acquiesced to Sarah's demand and evicted his own flesh and blood. A bossy wife can do damage that affects generations to come.

Hagar again found herself on her own, not knowing where to go. Abraham was greatly distressed, as her son was also his son. But God told Abraham to do what Sarah had asked, and promised that he would also make Ishmael into a great nation. And so Abraham sent Hagar and Ishmael off with a little food, a little water, and a lot of trust in God. He would have to endure another "sacrifice"—that of his son Isaac—at a later time. Both times required him to trust in God.

When the food and water ran out, Hagar despaired and began sobbing. Ishmael, thirsty and waiting to die, cried. God heard the cries. Again God spoke to Hagar, calling her by name. He told her not to be afraid. God not only cared for her physical needs, but he also cared about her emotional needs. He provided a well of water to refresh and nourish Hagar and her son. The only explanation for the well was that it came from God. God is a God who can make something from nothing.

Triumph through dysfunction

There are times throughout our lives when we will find ourselves in various dysfunctional situations. Perhaps it began in our biological family, and we are now alienated from family members. Or perhaps we have experienced ungodly actions or reactions within the church, as God's church is made up of imperfect people. Because of this, we may experience unfair treatment, harshness, or jealousy even from members of our spiritual family. When we endure dysfunction in relationships, we can be tempted to become disillusioned with God or his church. We may be tempted to become critical and bitter—wanting to make sure people "pay" for their actions toward us. While we need to be honest and call for love and kindness, it is never right to repay evil for evil.

Finally, all of you should be of one mind. Sympathize with each other. Love each other as brothers and sisters. Be tenderhearted, and keep a humble attitude. Don't repay evil for evil. Don't retaliate with insults when people insult you. Instead, pay them back with a blessing. That is what God has called you to do, and he will bless you for it. For the Scriptures say,

> "If you want to enjoy life
>   and see many happy days,
> keep your tongue from speaking evil
>   and your lips from telling lies.
> Turn away from evil and do good.
>   Search for peace, and work to maintain it.
> The eyes of the Lord watch over those who do right,
>   and his ears are open to their prayers.
> But the Lord turns his face
>   against those who do evil."

Now, who will want to harm you if you are eager to do good? But even if you suffer for doing what is right, God will reward you for it. So don't worry or be afraid of their threats. Instead, you must worship Christ as Lord of your life. And if someone asks about your Christian hope, always be ready to explain it.

(1 Peter 3:8–15, the New Living Translation)

Spiritual leaders don't crumble under pressure when faced with situations in which pride, jealousy, and other sinful actions spill over from others' hearts and mouths and affect their lives. Spiritual leaders come to believe that God sees their situation, just as Hagar did—and so they see God. They remember that God knows them by name and that with every temptation, he will provide a way of escape (1 Corinthians 10:13).

- When life or people treat you unfairly, what are ways you seek to "run away"?
- What difference does it make to know that God sees you when you are treated unfairly? Do you expect him to fix the unfairness, or do you ask him to help you trust him even through the difficulties?

- How do you respond when someone puts you down and treats you with harshness? Do you respond in kind, hoping to give them what they "deserve," or do you entrust yourself to God, who judges justly?
- When you feel stuck in a difficult situation, what can you do to find the way out?

Like Hagar, at first we may sob and we may be filled with despair. But she waited on God to act, and relied on his tender love and mercy. She went back when it was hard and held on to God's promise to her. She held on through the dysfunction, and (for better or worse) her life impacted an entire nation. The sin between Sarai and Hagar was not without effect—an effect we still see in the ongoing conflicts among the nations that emerged from their sons' descendants. Sin always has consequences. However, God's grace and mercy provide help in our time of need and are able to redeem us—even from ourselves. Spiritual leaders will keep going back to face tough circumstances, knowing God will provide an answer—in his timing. If we want to have an influence on generations to come, the key will be our faith: the faith to find and see God even through the confusion, pain, and inequity that life can bring.

Never take the "fun" out of dysfunction. Keep a sense of humor. And as Paul told Timothy, "Keep your head in all situations" (2 Timothy 4:5).
—Teresa Fontenot, Sydney, Australia

The scripture in Romans 3:4 (New Living Translation) has helped me through many dysfunctional situations: "Even if everyone else is a liar, God is true." God's word is still true, his plan for the church is still true, his love for his people and his desire to see the world saved all remain true, no matter how much we as people might mess up his perfect plan. Knowing this truth helps me to discern between "the baby and the bathwater." In other words, there are fundamental truths I must hold to, even when I am tempted to be disillusioned or disappointed with real life applications of these truths. God's word never disappoints. If I can keep holding on to his word, and holding out his word, I can navigate through rough waters.
—Jeanie Shaw, Burlington, Massachusetts

Galatians 6:9 refers to the type of faith that never gives up. If we keep sowing righteousness and building spiritual relationships, then churches can turn around, souls can be saved, and a harvest of righteousness will result. This takes lots of hard work, inspiring spiritual conversations, and a continual calling of people back to God's word.
—Caron Vassallo, Melbourne, Australia

PROFILE

Terry Axe, Virginia: Leadership Overcomes Dysfunction

by Kay McKean, Virginia

A child who has been a victim of shocking violence has to overcome many obstacles in this life. Such a child, through no fault of her own, has to struggle with guilt, fear, regret, and the never-ending question, *Why?* This is such a story.

At the tender age of six, Terry Axe and her mother and sister were living in what she recalls as a happy and loving home. One night, after being kissed good night and tucked into bed, Terry was startled to realize that there was an intruder in their home. With great fear, she watched as her mother was brutally stabbed to death by a man she had never seen before. After savagely attacking her mother, the man turned on her older sister and murdered her as well. Still in shock from what she witnessed, Terry realized that now the man was coming after her. For some reason, he put aside his knife, and instead of trying to kill her in the same way, he picked up a pair of Terry's leotards and wrapped them around her neck. Terry lost consciousness and remembers nothing more of that tragic night.

When she awoke, her world had changed. Her mother and sister were gone. Terry had to be placed in a witness protection program to protect her from the murderer, and could not even go to live with her father or other relatives. Terry eventually was able to testify in court, and the criminal was sentenced to prison. She continued to live with a foster family for several years. Finally, her father—who she had only known slightly until now—was able to gain custody, and she moved in with him. But the drama in Terry's life was not over.

At the age of eleven, Terry had a best friend who she played with and visited frequently. One day, her friend's brother took her aside and threatened her with a knife. Terry was shocked to realize that she was about to be raped. With no adults around to protect her, Terry endured the violent act with horror. Although he told her that if she told anyone she would be killed, Terry went straight home to tell her father.

What should have led to criminal prosecution ended in a simple "slap on the hand" for the young rapist. Although her father was dismayed at what had happened to his daughter, he was fearful that another barrage of court proceedings would be too much for the young girl, and with that rationale, the matter was dropped.

For Terry, this was too much to bear. Her life began to spin out of control. By the time she went to middle school, she was drinking heavily and smoking marijuana. In high school she became sexually active, living a life that was searching for love and peace in all the wrong places. Her guilt and regret were with her always. Crying herself to sleep at night, Terry asked the questions, Why? *Why was my mom taken from me at such a young time in my life? Why did I survive? Why did God leave me here to go through this pain and suffering?* These questions consumed her life, but she found no answers.

Finally, Terry decided that a change of scenery would help. She packed her bags and moved to California. Unfortunately, the change of location did not give her peace of mind. She found herself in the same routine of sex, drugs, and alcohol.

But Terry's questions and prayers were heard, although at first she was unaware. She met a man at her workplace who invited her to visit church with him and his wife. Although she can't remember exactly what the sermon was about that day, she remembers feeling hope for the first time in years, and she also remembers feeling a love that was different than anything she had ever felt before. As the Christian couple drove her home, she shared with tears her need for God. Terry began studying the Bible, and finally found the love of God that filled the deep hole in her heart.

After becoming a Christian, Terry's life was changed forever. She was so thankful to have a relationship with God and with true Christians. However, some of the questions of why still surfaced again and again. Even during the trial of her mother's murderer, there had been no clear answers as to why he had invaded their home and killed her loved ones. The questions and ambiguity of the situation haunted her at times. She wanted answers, but they were not there.

Finally, after much prayer, study of God's word, and help from disciples, Terry was able to come to peace about the unanswered questions in her life. She realized that suffering is in this world because of sin. But she also came to the conviction that God has worked and continues to work through the suffering in her life to bring her to him. Suffering brought her to her knees and caused her to cry out to God. Terry also learned that God went through suffering—letting his only Son die on a cross for her sins—to show her that God understands her pain.

Although Terry's early life was filled with violence and pain, her life is now filled with glorifying God. Terry is a natural "nurturer," and she loves others deeply. She is able to feel deeply for the sins and sorrows of others. She is also able to point others to the God who saved her and gave her eternal life. Terry loves the promises of Romans 5:2–5: "And we rejoice in the hope of the glory of God. Not only so, but we also rejoice in our sufferings, because we know that suffering produces perseverance; perseverance, character; and character, hope. And hope does not disappoint us." Terry's life serves as a reminder that no matter what, God is available to help, comfort, strengthen, and ultimately bring us all to eternal life!

Terry is a member of the Northern Virginia Church of Christ. She leads the women in a singles' family group and is a vital part of that congregation.

CHAPTER TWENTY-FOUR

Priscilla: Leadership and Teamwork
Jeanie Shaw

Acts 18

Priscilla was walking by the field near her home on a sunny day. She prayed as she walked, praising God and requesting wisdom and awareness of the people around her who still needed to hear the great news about Jesus. She noticed two oxen yoked together, plowing the field she was passing. They worked together in perfect rhythm—as if they were listening to the same song as they worked. She laughed as her vivid imagination pictured the havoc that would ensue if one of the oxen were to be yoked together with a rooster or a pig. Frustration would abound—and the field would never get plowed. She smiled as she thought about her husband, Aquila. While she didn't think of him (or herself) as an ox, she thought of the pleasure they enjoyed as they worked together side by side for the Lord. Like the oxen that were yoked, she felt they had found a rhythm in their work. And they were, in fact, listening to the same song. It was God's salvation song, and it was beautiful.

She recounted the first time she and Aquila had met their friend Paul. They had all moved to Corinth, where they shared a common occupation—tent-making. This friendship had changed their lives. Though they all worked hard together making and repairing tents, they had also found a purpose far greater than fashioning temporary housing. They were able to offer to others what they themselves had found—an eternal home.

Paul, a Pharisee before he was converted to Jesus' ways, had a deep knowledge of the Scriptures. He had quickly come to realize how the Scriptures all pointed to Jesus. His convictions were rock solid, and his ability to teach and refute lies had garnered the attention and respect of many, including Priscilla and Aquila. How deeply Priscilla cherished the times Paul had spent in their home, and the many hours the three of them had spent sharing Scriptures, praying, strategizing, and dreaming of doors that would open for the good news. While Priscilla and her husband continued to make their living by making tents, their occupation was overshadowed by their preoccupation—letting the whole world know about Jesus.

The joy of teamwork

Priscilla loved the life she lived beside her husband. They purposely shared their home and their lives with people, along with the good news of Jesus. As they gave to others, they keenly felt the truth of Jesus' promise—that it is more blessed to give than to receive (Acts 20:35). They simply could not out-give God. In their marriage, they experienced the harmony that grew from their united convictions and discipleship. It was a joy to open up their home to the church each week as the Christians came together to worship. While it was extra work to have the entire church in her home, Priscilla considered it a great honor and privilege to host the family of God.

From time to time, she and Aquila traveled to Ephesus and Rome to assist their friend Paul in his preaching and teaching. Why wouldn't they? What could be more important than helping others find a relationship with the only one who had the words of eternal life?

Spiritual leaders like Priscilla understand that functioning as a team is more effective than operating solo. For those who are married, there is no more important teammate than your spouse. Priscilla and Aquila worked together as a team. Your children are also an important part of your "team living for Jesus." If you segment your "spiritual life" from your family life, your spiritual life will become more like a club membership than a way of life. Do your rides together in the car, your dinner times, your fun times all include conversations about Jesus? Do you regularly have people in your home with whom you are sharing your faith? Do you pray together for the church and for open doors with your neighbors, your children's teachers, and the parents of your children's friends? This is all part of building a "family team" for Jesus—much like Priscilla and Aquila did within their marriage. As you work together in your marriage and family, you demonstrate the unity for which Jesus died. There is no greater comparison of Jesus and the church than a loving, purposeful, selfless, and united marriage (Ephesians 5:21-33). As your family serves Jesus together, your children learn what is most valuable, and how to seek first the kingdom of God. They learn that while life does not center around them, they are still needed, valued, and important. In order for a marriage and a family to work as team, there must be planning together, prayer together, deliberate family growth, times set for relationships, and joyful hospitality.

If you are single, it can be a joy to function with your household and your close friends as a spiritual team. If you are single and hoping to be married, I plead with you to not compromise by settling for a relationship with a man who does not share your deep convictions about God and his ways. Throughout Scripture, God has made clear his design for marriage, and his command that his people not be unequally yoked. Certainly, when members of a team are not united in their goals, the team becomes weak and unsuccessful. However, when a team shares a common purpose, there is no limit to what can be accomplished with the help of God's power.

If you are married, but your spouse has not yet become a Christian, you face a challenge, yes—but it is a challenge that many Christian women have learned to successfully navigate, remaining faithful to God while staying close to their husbands. (I hope you will find encouragement from the profiles in this book that highlight your sisters in Christ who have learned to thrive in this very situation.) It is vital for you to find close spiritual relationships that help you and your husband find ways to function together rather than alone.

No matter what your situation, always remember that God is your most important team member. He is the captain of all our teams, whether we are married or single. You can have a great effect on others as you help them grow closer to God.

The perils of working independently and benefits of working together

When we are leading, it often feels more complicated to work with a team. Collaboration takes time and energy. But without teamwork, not only do we fail to see our own blind spots, but it is more difficult to overcome our timidity and fear. We get lonely when we try to function as an independent leader. Leaders who don't surround themselves with a team often struggle with a sense of self-importance—as if everything depends on them—or a sense of inadequacy, as their weaknesses are all too evident. A team keeps you from feeling over-responsible when things don't go well, and from being overconfident and taking credit when things go well. When you lead without a team surrounding you, you are limited by your own faith and abilities—and the people around you don't feel needed. God tells us everyone is needed. It behooves us all to help them feel that way.

As Priscilla worked together with her husband, they were effective in sharing their faith. In Acts 18:24–28, we read about how Priscilla and Aquila helped a great teacher named Apollos to have a better understanding of Jesus' ways. Alone, Priscilla and Aquila may have lacked the courage or the clarity of mind to approach Apollos, who was eloquent and well-versed in the Scriptures, but still missing an accurate understanding of God's plan of salvation. But together, not only did they invite him into their home, but they also taught him the truth more accurately, and he in turn used that teaching to help save many souls. As a team, Priscilla and Aquila were able to feed off of each other's strengths. The people around them who became disciples were added to their team, thus making more and more impact for Jesus.

Crucial team values

Effective team functioning includes good communication that goes "both ways." Spiritual leaders listen well and don't love their own opinion too much. Understand that each of us brings to the team our own life stories, baggage, prejudices, and hurts that color the way we view things. It is crucial that we learn how to express ourselves and yet submit to the group. Each member of a team is important, and each member needs to possess deep biblical convictions, godly character, competence, and chemistry (the ability to work well with others).

Priscilla was focused on other people. She did not seek worldly or selfish pursuits. She was focused on pleasing her God and helping others find him, always alert to ways to serve.

As a spiritual leader, never lose sight of your purpose as a team. Spiritual leaders don't build a team just for the sake of building a team, but for the purpose of loving God and loving people—helping as many as possible to make it to heaven.

- What qualities do you notice in teams that are harmonious and successful?
- Do you tend to work independently, or do you value teamwork? As you grow in spiritual leadership, what are some ways you could decide to work in or with a team? What contributions might you make to the team?
- If you are married, what are practical ways you can work side by side for the Lord in your marriage? Discuss with your spouse (or household or close friends, if you are single) one change you can make to become more effective as a team.
- Think of some practical ways you can help your children understand that your family works together as a team that serves Jesus.

We may think we are a great team player. But do the people around us and the people we work with see us as a team player? How would people in your family or your small group in the church describe your character, convictions, competence, and chemistry as they work with you? You will never know unless you ask them. Be courageous and ask them for their honest evaluation of the way you function in a team.

Tradition tells us that Priscilla and Aquila sacrificed their lives for Jesus' sake. In the tradition of the Roman Church, on a July eighth, Priscilla and Aquila were led out of the city and beheaded because they taught that Jesus was Lord. Whether or not this tradition is true, they certainly lived lives that denied themselves for the sake of the Gospel. If it is true, their relationship could be described using the powerful lyrics from the song "Remember the Lord" from the musical *Upside Down*. In this song, Peter's wife Abby persuades Peter to keep his faith rather than deny Jesus in order to save her from martyrdom. Perhaps Priscilla could have also sung to Aquila:

> "Don't you dare even give a thought of saving me today,
> I'm already saved, and for that gift there's no price I won't pay.
> So get behind me Satan, the devil's last chance slips away...
> Remember where your treasure's stored...
> Remember the Lord!"[25]

May we live like Priscilla, giving ourselves wholly to those working with us—united and purpose-filled to the glory of God.

Recognize and appreciate the different strengths you have in your marriage. It takes time to listen to each other's perspective on ministry, family, etc. It takes time and work to be a team.

—Anita Allen, Hartford, Connecticut

I have had to learn to turn envy and intimidation into admiration and collaboration. This is made possible by appreciating our differences in the body, and working to help each person have confidence in her God-given gifts.

—Mary Lou Craig, Boonton, New Jersey

Teamwork is God's plan. Teamwork ensures success, and the success is shared by everyone on the team. It encourages openness as well as new and exciting ideas.

—Sally Hooper, Dallas, Texas

"Two are better than one" (Ecclesiastes 4:9). How refreshing it is to know that I don't have to have all the answers or have to do it all perfectly myself! Instead I can do what I do best and find and use the sisters around me to do what they do best. Working together, we make a much better picture of Jesus.

—Geri Laing, Lake Worth, Florida

Include your children as part of the family team that serves Jesus and brings others to him.

—Jeanie Shaw, Burlington, Massachusetts

PROFILE

Pat Morr, International Missionary: Teamwork

by Nadine Templer, New Delhi, India

As I write this article from my home in New Delhi, India, I think of the many women who have inspired me over the years. Our churches are full of mature women who have devoted their lives to serving God and his people—some at greater cost than others.

Pat Morr is one of my heroes. I first met her when I was a young woman, newly married in London, and about to embark on the greatest adventure of my life: moving to the mission field of India.

Phil and Pat Morr served as missionaries throughout their entire married life. Together they served in England, China, Australia, Hong Kong, Vietnam, Ireland, and their home country, the United States. Their teamwork in spreading the good news of Jesus is inspiring and exemplary. Pat is now seventy-six years old and still serving God. She was recently widowed when Phil, her husband of many years, passed away. As those who knew Phil best would expect, he was serving on the mission field in India when he became ill. He returned home to the States, and went to be with Jesus soon after.

Phil and Pat have five children—two biological, and three adopted. All are disciples and are raising families in the Lord. They are incredible testimonies to the lives of their parents. Pat's daughter Wendy says this about her mom, "She has inspired me to be the person I am today. I am so grateful to know Christ as my Savior and have a serving heart. I know that her example and teachings have led me to be who I am today."

Pat's devotion to God is obvious by the way she followed her husband around the world with young children and teenagers in tow. They never had a lot of money, but they served people with all their heart. I remember hearing Pat share that her children would go to sleep at night listening to their parents studying the Bible with people in the next room.

Pat is also known for her hospitality. She is a great cook and homemaker. Phil and Pat would always entertain people in their home. That is no easy task with a large family—especially a large family with limited resources on the mission field.

At the age when most people would be enjoying their retirement, Phil and Pat (at the ages of seventy and sixty-eight, respectively) were called to lead a church in Grand Rapids, Michigan. They led with a zeal and faith that could put some young people to shame.

Another thing that struck me about Pat over the years was her humility and her gentle and quiet spirit. She always gave glory to God and was quick to praise others.

Soon after Phil passed away, she moved to be with her children who lead a church in Indiana. As expected, Pat quickly became fully engaged in the women's ministry in her new city, teaching and counseling many other women. I am sure many could write more about Pat, but I will conclude with the following words spoken a few years ago by a friend of the Morr family, which Pat's daughter shared with me: "Phil Morr has become widely known for his dedicated and successful evangelistic zeal. Without Pat's cooperation, however, he likely would not be preaching at all, much less spreading the gospel in remote and difficult areas where he has chosen to serve. All who have done such work have been able to do so only because of wives who were willing to cooperate and go with them. Many a man has been limited in what he could do because of a wife who did not share his dedication."

Pat never held back. The question for her has never been "Why?" but rather "Why not?"

Appendix

Supplement to Chapter 19, The Women of Romans 16
Defining and Clarifying Roles and Relational Expectations
Jeanie Shaw

In chapter 19, we discussed the importance of relationships, yet at times we get confused as to difference types of relationships we need to have and practice.

Sometimes terminology gets us into trouble: We use a particular word to describe our relationship with someone, but the word means something different to us than it does to them. Our expectations for the relationship are different, and feelings get hurt. In attempting to better describe roles, responsibilities, and relationships in our church family, it may be helpful to clarify some relationship terminology.

Discipling:

This term calls to mind a vast variety of experiences and history. I would define a discipling relationship as a *whole-life approach of involvement, transparency, and input between two disciples of Jesus.*

A discipling relationship may involve an equal, two-way dynamic between people of common age, stage of life, and role within the church. I'm not talking about a vague, "Hey, we're friends, so let's sometimes ask each other how we're doing," kind of friendship, but a committed relationship where we consistently meet together with the specific intention of helping one another to grow.

What might this look like on a day-to-day basis? Such a relationship would involve consistent and deliberate time to share, discuss, and evaluate personal life decisions, priorities, and schedule, aimed at discerning what is best for spiritual growth and effectiveness.

How do we choose a person to engage in a discipling relationship? For every church, the answer will be different. Some church members choose their own discipling relationships based on friendship and geographic closeness; some church staffs help their members find a suitable discipling relationship, perhaps based on members' particular ministry within the church.

A discipling relationship between people in leadership roles may include a supervisory responsibility (for example, a women's ministry leader overseeing the progress and work of an intern or younger staff member), or it might involve a mutually shared desire between leaders with similar maturity, to help one another to do and be our best for God.

Do you have this kind of relationship, and if so, with whom?

Mentoring:

Mentor is not as popular a term in our family of churches, but it describes a fresh and somewhat different dynamic—it would probably consist of less frequent, but still very purposeful, involvement. It implies a need for one person to pass on specific expertise to a person who desires it. A mentoring relationship would be less "whole-life" and more "role-specific" in scope and focus. The depth of the friendship would be less of a focus than acquiring and imparting needed skills, competence, and wisdom in a certain area. People desiring to serve in certain leadership roles might desire and be expected to set up a mentoring relationship with a more experienced role model. This is common practice in seminaries for students, who are paired with practicing ministers or pastors.

While there can be some overlap between discipling and mentoring in general, remember that a discipling relationship would be more comprehensive, involving familiarity and input on a whole-life basis, while a mentoring relationship would involve a specific role or area of expertise. Discipling would be more of a partnership and a two-way relationship, whereas mentorship clearly involves a teacher and a student. When entering into a mentor-type relationship, it would be wise to discuss the expectations for the relationship. Both people should understand the scope of the relationship, and what specific areas of expertise the mentor is trying to pass on to the mentees.

We all need mentoring in different areas of our life, at different stages of our life. In our student years, we may need mentoring in our studies, or time management skills. When we are first leading a Bible discussion group, we may need mentoring in how to plan a class and lead a discussion. When we are preparing to be married, we may seek mentoring in our relationship in the form of premarital counseling. If we are training to fulfill a certain role in the church (like becoming an elder's wife), we may need mentoring. And the list goes on!

Do you have a mentor in a certain area of your life, and are you mentoring another person?

Best friendships:

Best friend is a term that causes more misunderstanding and disappointment than any other relationship term we use! We've all experienced this—wanting or expecting to be someone's best friend, and having hurt feelings when they don't reciprocate. And of course, the very term itself presents a problem: *"best friend"* implies that you can only have one.

In the past, in our fellowship, any discipling or mentoring relationship was also expected to become a best friend relationship—talk about a lot of pressure in one relationship! This is, of course, impossible; it almost always guarantees disappointment at best, and disillusionment and bitterness at worst. I suggest we use the term "best friendship" with caution. When we are speaking of discipling and mentoring relationships, a wiser and more realistic expectation would be this: to be "the best friend I can be" for what this relationship can and should be.

What does that mean in the real world? It means that I can be a friend to the people I mentor, but there will be limits to what our relationship can involve. If I only see them once a month, then friendship-building activities such as going to dinner or the movies, or making regular phone calls to chat, would be unlikely, and thus not expected. The degree of contact and focus of our defined relationship would then dictate reasonable expectations—an expectation to be "the best friend that the relationship reasonably allows." Evolving dynamics of depth and friendship should be discussed "as we go." Otherwise, misaligned expectations can create unintended conflict or hurt feelings.

Training:

Training would most often fall under the purview of a mentoring relationship like the kind mentioned in the discussion of mentoring. Training would be most often practiced in roles of leadership or service, and would serve the purpose of teaching, modeling, and evaluating progress in specific skills and competencies. These should be measurable and relevant to the tasks and functions that a particular role demands (such as leading a Bible discussion group, studying the Bible with someone, taking on a deacon or deaconess role, leading a specific ministry, or being a teacher). For the men, becoming an elder or evangelist would require specific training, including a training relationship where it is clearly recognized who is the trainer and who is the trainee.

Equipping:

This is a parallel term to training, though in our church culture it is more often applied to the responsibility of church leadership to equip church members in basic disciplines of discipleship such as evangelism, prayer, one-another relationships, and other acts of service in body life. However we may define *equipping*, the Scriptures are clear: leaders are not supposed to do all the work of the ministry themselves while everyone else watches. Leaders are called "to prepare God's people for works of service, so that the body of Christ may be built up" (Ephesians 4:12). And of course, in order to equip others, we ourselves must continue to be equipped, which means we must maintain a continual learner's spirit.

For all: a call to honesty, humility, and kindness

As women who strive to serve and lead in various ways in God's church, we will all fill different roles at different times in our lives. Each role will require humility, confidence, selflessness, and love. No matter what role or roles you currently play, these scriptures can guide your heart and attitude, and teach you how to have successful relationships.

> Be completely humble and gentle; be patient, bearing with one another in love. (Ephesians 4:2)

> Instead, speaking the truth in love, we will in all things grow up into him who is the Head, that is, Christ. From him the whole body, joined and held together by every supporting ligament, grows and builds itself up in love, as each part does its work. (Ephesians 4:15–16)

> To the Jews who had believed him, Jesus said, "If you hold to my teaching, you are really my disciples. Then you will know the truth, and the truth will set you free." (John 8:31–32)

> They came to him and said, "Teacher, we know you are a man of integrity. You aren't swayed by men, because you pay no attention to who they are; but you teach the way of God in accordance with the truth. Is it right to pay taxes to Caesar or not?" (Mark 12:14)

> There is no fear in love. But perfect love drives out fear, because fear has to do with punishment. The one who fears is not made perfect in love. (1 John 4:18)

Whether we are leading or following, training or being trained, our spirit and attitude will make all the difference in our relationships. As the Scriptures state in Ephesians 4:2, humility, gentleness, and patience are crucial in our conversations. These qualities will ensure that everyone feels respected, valued, and loved. As we grow in our relationships, we will be better able to carry out Jesus' deepest desire for our lives—to love God with all our heart, soul, and mind, and to love our neighbor as ourselves (Matthew 22:36–39). And as we grow in our love for God, we will be better able to love each other—and ourselves.

Humility

Leaders must take personal responsibility for being easy to approach when people have questions or concerns. People feel they can approach us when our humility, gentleness, and love are evident. Jesus, who had all of these qualities, was easily approached by sinners, elders, children, rich people, and poor people. In fact, in Matthew 11:28, he pleads for us all to come to him and find rest for our souls.

Honesty

Honesty—speaking the truth in love—is also God's plan and call for each of us. Satan wants nothing more than to keep us from being honest with each other. I struggled for years with speaking the truth in love. I would say things in such a way that I'd *almost* say something, but it was nearly impossible for people to decipher the hints of what I felt. I had learned, through unfortunate situations where I tried to be honest and it didn't go well, to just be quiet and hold things in. But "stuffing things" severely hampers open, vulnerable relationships. I had to learn and practice, with the help of others, how to be honest and say what was truly inside my heart. I had stuffed for so long that at first I didn't even know what I felt. We need honesty in order to lead, to follow, and to love. No matter what your role in the church, honesty will determine the quality of your relationships.

But speaking honestly takes wisdom, tact, and a good sense of timing. It is also important to understand that there may be some pieces missing in our understanding of any given situation. I've learned to ask questions—a lot of them—before speaking, especially if I only have one-sided information.

Gentleness and kindness

Gentleness and kindness (or niceness) are also qualities God instructs us to practice. It is of utmost importance to remember that God is a God of grace and mercy. While he is just, he is also merciful. He is perfectly grace and truth. A constant prayer I pray is to better know how to meld God's grace and truth in my everyday relationships. I love how the Apostle John, as he spent time with Jesus, progressed from a "Son of Thunder" (Mark 3:17) to "the Apostle of love" (see 1 John). When I don't know how to interact in a relationship, I try to remember that "mercy triumphs over judgment" (James 2:13) and that God has continually bestowed immeasurable mercy on me.

I pray that these practical definitions can help you become more effective at loving others as Jesus loves. As we learn to "play well with others on the playground" and become better team players, we can more effectively pray alongside Jesus the prayer he prayed—

> "My prayer is not for them alone. I pray also for those who will believe in me through their message, that all of them may be one, Father, just as you are in me and I am in you. May they also be in us so that the world may believe that you have sent me. I have given them the glory that you gave me, that they may be one as we are one: I in them and you in me. May they be brought to complete unity to let the world know that you sent me and have loved them even as you have loved me." (John 17:20–23)

Let us pray toward this end.

End Notes

Chapter 2, Tabitha: Leadership and Example
[1]Blue Letter Bible Online, s.v. "πλήρησ," accessed March 26, 2014, http://www.blueletterbible.org/lang/lexicon/lexicon.cfm?strongs=G4134&t=NIV.
[2]Blue Letter Bible Online, s.v. "ἡγέομαι," accessed March 26, 2014, http://www.blueletterbible.org/lang/lexicon/lexicon.cfm?strongs=G2233&t=NIV.
[3]Blue Letter Bible Online, s.v. "δοῦλοσ," accessed March 26, 2014, http://www.blueletterbible.org/lang/lexicon/lexicon.cfm?strongs=G1401&t=NIV.

Chapter 3, Hannah: Leadership and Vulnerability
[4]Online Etymology Dictionary, s. v. "courage," accessed April 25, 2014, ihttp://www.etymonline.com/index.php?allowed_in_frame=0&search=courage&searchmode=none.
[5]Brené Brown, *I Thought It Was Just Me (but it isn't): Making the Journey from "What Will People Think" to "I Am Enough"* (New York: Gotham Books, 2007).

Chapter 4, Sarah: Leadership and Courage
[6]Dictionary.com, s.v. "courage," accessed April 25, 2014, http://dictionary.reference.com/browse/courage?s=t.
[7]Jewish Encyclopedia.com, s.v. "Sarah," accessed April 29, 2014, www.jewishencyclopedia.com/articles/13194-sarah-sarai.

Chapter 5, The Sinful Woman: Leadership and Gratitude
[8]Robert Emmons, "How Gratitude Can Help You Through Hard Times" on The Greater Good Science Center Web site, the University of California at Berkeley, accessed May 2, 2014, http://greatergood.berkeley.edu/article/item/how_gratitude_can_help_you_through_hard_times?utm_source=GG+Newsletter+%232+-+May+2013&utm_campaign=GG+Newsletter+-+May+2013&utm_medium=email.

Chapter 9, Martha: Leadership and Hospitality
[9]Miriam Feinberg Vamosh. *Food At The Time of the Bible* (Herzlia: Palphot, Ltd., 2007), 27.
[10]Widely attributed to second-century rabbi Yose ben Yoezer. Quoted by Ann Spangler and Lois Tverberg in *Sitting at the Feet of Rabbi Jesus* (Grand Rapids: Zondervan, 2009), 14.
[11]Joseph H. Thayer, *Thayer's Greek-English Lexicon of the New Testament* (Grand Rapids: Zondervan, 1956), Greek word "philoxenia."

Chapter 10, Abigail, Leadership and Prudence
[12] "The Gambler," by Don Schlitz. Recorded by Kenny Rogers, 1978.

Chapter 12, Esther, Leadership and Vision
[13] The Midrash states "that Esther's father died during her mother's pregnancy, and the latter died during childbirth (*Esther Rabbah* 6:5; BT *Megillah* 13a)." Tamar Meir, "Esther: Midrash and Aggadah," *Jewish Women: A Comprehensive Historical Encyclopedia*, March 20, 2009. Jewish Women's Archive. Viewed on April 29, 2014. http:// wa.org/encyclopedia/article/esther-midrash-and-aggadah.

[14] See Esther 2:10–11.

[15] Matthew Henry. *Matthew Henry's Commentary on the Whole Bible: Complete and Unabridged in One Volume* (Peabody: Hendrickson, 1994).

[16] Ibid.

[17] John Boardman et al., eds., *The Cambridge Ancient History Volume 3, Part 2: The Assyrian and Babylonian Empires and Other States of the Near East, from the Eighth to the Sixth Centuries BC, 2nd ed.* (Cambridge: Cambridge University Press, 1991), 198.

[18] For a great explanation of this insight, see Gloria Baird's book, *God's Pitcher and Other Spiritual Thoughts* (Spring Hill: DPI, 2008).

Chapter 13, The Canaanite Woman: Leadership and Boldness
[19] Dictionary.com, s.v. "boldness," accessed April 29, 2014, http://dictionary.reference.com/browse/boldness?s=t.

Chapter 14, Lydia: Leadership and Persuasion
[20] "The Jewish population at Philippi must have been limited, for there was no synagogue there; ten Jewish males were required for a synagogue. **A place of prayer** (cf. v. 16), which may have been a place in the open air or a simple building, was located by the Gangites River about a mile and one-half west of town." *The Bible Knowledge Commentary: An Exposition of the Scriptures*, eds. J. F. Walvoord and R. B. Zuck (Wheaton: Victor Books, 1985), Acts section.

[21] J. Strong, *Enhanced Strong's Lexicon*. Accessed via Logos Bible Software (Bellingham, WA: 2001).

[22] Joseph H. Thayer, *Thayer's Greek-English Lexicon of the New Testament* (Grand Rapids: Zondervan, 1956), s.v. "παρακαλέω." Blue Letter Bible Online, s.v. "παρακαλέω," accessed April 29, 2014, http://www.blueletterbible.org/lang/lexicon/lexicon.cfm?Strongs=G3870&t=KJV

[23] Gerhard Kittel and Gerhard Friedrich, *Theological Dictionary of the New Testament, Vol. 5* (Stuttgart: Wm. B. Eerdmans Publishing Co., 1976), 740.

Chapter 15, Miriam: Leadership and Initiative
[24]"This Little Light of Mine" by Harry Dixon Loes, circa 1920.

Chapter 24, Priscilla: Leadership and Teamwork
[25]"Remember the Lord" from the musical *Upside Down*. Music and Lyrics by Steven L. Johnson and Sherwin Mackintosh, 1987. Cited with permission.

Fruity Tunes
Jeanie Shaw
ISBN: 978-1477609040
$7.99

There's a Turkey at Your Door
Jeanie Shaw
ISBN: 978-1479340125
$12.99

Jacob's Journey
Jeanie Shaw
ISBN: 978-1577821618
$9.99

**Available at
www.ipibooks.com**

Prime Rib
Jeanie Shaw
ISBN: 978-1494292928
$11.99

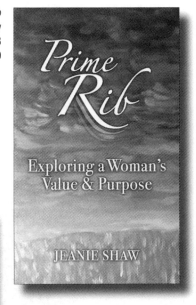

My Morning Cup
Jeanie Shaw
ISBN: 978-157782259-2
$9.99

Understanding Goose
Jeanie Shaw
ISBN: 978-1463689582
$11.99

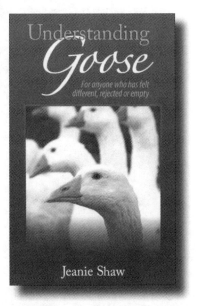

**Available at
www.ipibooks.com**

www.ipibooks.com